Crochet Holiday Collection™

the Needlecraft Shop®

Product Development Director
Andy Ashley

Publishing Services Manager
Ange Van Arman

Crochet Design Manager
Deborah Levy-Hamburg

Product Development Staff
**Mickie Akins, Darla Hassell,
Sandra Miller Maxfield, Alice
Mitchell, Elizabeth Ann White**

Editor
Donna Scott

Assistant Editor
Sharon Lothrop

Crochet Editorial Staff
**Shirley Brown, Liz Field,
Nina Marsh, Lyne Pickens**

Book Design/Supervisor
Minette Smith

Production Artist
Debby Keel

Photography Supervisor
Scott Campbell

Photographer
Andy J. Burnfield

Photo Stylist
Martha Coquat

Production Coordinator
Glenda Chamberlain

Library of Congress
Cataloging-in-Publication Data
ISBN: 1-57367-118-5
First Printing: 2001
Library of Congress Catalog Card Number:
2001090473
Published and Distributed by
**The Needlecraft Shop,
Big Sandy, Texas 75755**
NeedlecraftShop.com

Printed in the United States of America

Dear Friends,

When asked to think about the special
occasions that have taken place in my life, certain
key events spring to mind. Most of these are tied
together in some way with what I would consider
milestones. The patterns chosen for this book were
carefully selected while I was reliving some of
those precious memories. Most of these will mean
different things to each of us, but the common
denominator will still be one of presenting family
and friends with the here-and-now, wrapped up
in the mists of nostalgia.

How about bringing home baby for the first
time? How small he seemed. How frightening
the feeling of responsibility! The contentment felt
holding him cuddled into his special baby afghan,
wearing the booties grandma crocheted for him on
his tiny little feet. Fast forward to watching those
same feet walk across the stage to receive the
parchment that is a stepping stone to adulthood—
high school graduation.

We all like to sit and contemplate flashes of
special times spent together, whether it's seeing
who gets a pinch for not wearing green on St.
Patrick's Day to the youngest member of the family
helping Daddy cut the Thanksgiving turkey for the
first time. All of these create a mental slide show
we will never be tired of seeing over and over
throughout the years. Keep these memories close to
your heart while you crochet reminders of the past
and anticipation for the future.

Donna

Donna Scott
Editor

Contents

Chapter One
Afghans for the Holidays

Chapter Two
Gifts for the Holidays

Chapter Three
Holiday Fun

Chapter Four

Holidays in a Hurry

Chapter Five

Holidays Room by Room

Chapter One

Afghans for the Holidays

Whether you are home for the holidays, in route to visit family and friends, or simply looking for a gift to create a special memory, we have an afghan just right for the occasion. From welcoming the spring holiday season to the joy of Christmas during winter, keep your crochet close at hand.

Ducks on Parade

Designed by Lou Ann Millsaps

Finished Size

Afghan is 35" x 51".

Materials

- ○ 3-ply sport yarn — 18 oz. yellow, 11 oz. lavender, Small amount orange
- ○ 4 yds. purple ¼" satin picot ribbon
- ○ Tapestry needle
- ○ F and G crochet hooks or sizes needed to obtain gauges

Gauges

With **F hook**, 9 sc sts = 2"; 9 sc rows = 2". With **G hook**, 4 sc sts = 1"; 4 sc rows = 1".

Notes: When changing colors (see page 158), always drop yarn to wrong side of work. Use a separate skein or ball of yarn for each color section. Do not carry yarn across from one section to another. Fasten off colors at end of each color section.

Each square on graph equals one sc.

Work odd-numbered graph rows from right to left; work even-numbered rows from left to right.

Use G hook unless otherwise stated.

Solid Square (make 7)

Row 1: With yellow, ch 45, sc in 2nd ch from hook, sc in each ch across, turn (44).

Rows 2-38: Ch 1, sc in each st across, turn. At the end of last row, **do not turn**.

Rnd 39: Working around outer edge, with F hook, ch 1, sc in end of each row and in each st around with 3 sc in each corner st, join with sl st in first sc, fasten off.

Duck Square (make 8)

Row 1: With lavender, ch 45, sc in 2nd ch from hook, sc in each ch across, turn (44).

Rows 2-38: Ch 1, sc in each st across changing colors according to graph, turn. At end of last row, **do not turn,** fasten off.

Rnd 39: With F hook and yellow, join with sc in any st, sc in each st and in end of each row around with 3 sc in each corner st, join with sl st in first sc, fasten off.

Alternating Duck Squares and Solid Squares, sew together in 3 rows of 5 squares each as shown in photo.

Edging

Rnd 1: With right side of afghan facing you, with F hook and lavender, join with sc in any st, sc in each st around with 3 sc in each center corner st, join with sl st in first sc.

Rnd 2: Sl st in each st around, join with sl st in first sl st, fasten off.

Cut ribbon into 9" pieces; tie one piece into a bow around each duck's neck. •

☐ = Lavender   ▨ = Yellow   ▦ = Orange

DUCK GRAPH

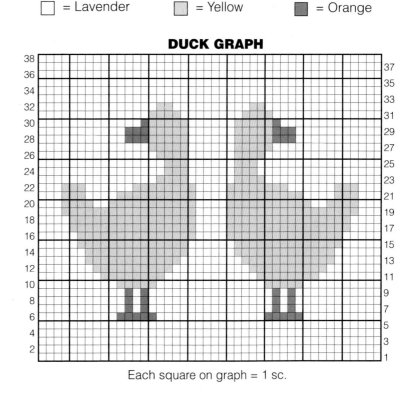

Each square on graph = 1 sc.

Heavenly Angels

Designed by Sue Childress

Finished Size

Blanket is 37" x 40". Dress fits 11" tall doll.

Materials for Baby Blanket

- ○ 3-ply sport yarn — 27 oz. cream
- ○ Tapestry needle
- ○ F crochet hook or size needed to obtain gauge

Materials for Doll

- ○ 3-ply sport yarn — 6 oz. cream
- ○ Fabric paint — blue, black, white, and pink
- ○ 11"– tall cloth doll
- ○ 2¼ yds. cream ¼" satin ribbon
- ○ Blonde curly doll hair
- ○ Pink powder blush
- ○ Small paintbrush
- ○ Pink powder blush
- ○ Craft glue or hot glue gun
- ○ Fabric stiffener
- ○ Tapestry needle
- ○ F crochet hook or size needed to obtain gauge

Gauge

5 dc sts = 1"; 2 dc rows = 1". One shell = 1" across; 5 shell rows = 3".

Blanket

Notes: For **block,** dc in next ch and in next dc, or, dc in next 2 dc.

For **ending block (end block),** dc in each of last 2 dc.

For **beginning block (beg block),** ch 3, dc in each of next 2 dc.

For **mesh,** ch 1, skip next dc or next ch-1 sp, dc in next dc.

Row 1: Ch 183, dc in 4th ch from hook, dc in each ch across, turn (181 dc).

Rows 2-96: Work according to graph (on page 13) across, turn. At end of last row, **do not turn.**

Rnd 97: For **border,** working around outer edge, ch 1, 2 sc in end of each row and sc in each st around with 3 sc in each corner st, join with sl st in first sc (754).

Rnd 98: Ch 3, 4 dc in same st, skip next st, sc in next st, skip next st, *5 dc in next st, skip next 2 sts, sc in next st, skip next 2 sts; repeat from * around, join with sl st in top of ch-3, fasten off.

Dress

Notes: For **shell,** (2 dc, ch 1, 2 dc) in next st or sp.

For **double shell (dbl shell),** (2 dc, ch 1, 2 dc, ch 1, 2 dc) in next st or sp.

For **beginning shell (beg shell),** ch 3, (dc, ch 1, 2 dc) in same st or sp.

Row 1: Starting at **neckline,** ch 32, dc in 4th ch from hook, dc in next 5 chs, 3 dc in next ch, dc in next 14 chs, 3 dc in next ch, dc in last 7 chs, turn (34 dc).

Row 2: Ch 3, dc in next 7 sts, shell in next st, dc in next 16 sts, shell in next st, dc in last 8

sts, turn (32 dc, 2 shells).

Row 3: Ch 3, dc in same st, skip next dc, (shell in next dc, skip next dc) 3 times, dbl shell in ch sp of next shell, skip last 2 dc of same shell, (shell in next dc, skip next dc) 8 times, dbl shell in ch sp of next shell, skip last 2 dc of same shell, skip next dc, (shell in next dc, skip next dc) 3 times, 2 dc in last dc, turn (14 shells, 4 dc, 2 dbl shells).

Row 4: Ch 3, dc in same st, shell in ch sp of each shell and dbl shell in ch sp of each dbl shell across to last 2 dc, skip next dc, 2 dc in last dc, turn (14 shells, 4 dbl shells, 4 dc).

Rnd 5: Working in rnds, ch 3, dc in same st, shell each of next 3 shells; for **armhole,** ch 4, skip next 2 dbl shells; shell in each of next 8 shells; for **armhole,** ch 4, skip next 2 dbl shells, shell in each of next 3 shells, 2 dc in last dc, ch 1, join with sl st in top of ch-3, **do not turn** (14 shells, 2 ch-4 sps).

Rnd 6: Sl st in next 3 dc, sl st in next ch sp, beg shell, shell in each of next 2 shells, shell in 2nd ch of next ch-4 sp, shell in each of next 8 shells, shell in 2nd ch of next ch-4 sp, shell in each of next 3 shells, shell in last ch-1 sp on last rnd, join (17 shells).

Rnd 7: Ch 3, dc in each dc and in each ch-1 sp of each shell around, join (85 dc).

Continued on page 12

Heavenly Angels

Continued from page 10

Rnd 8: Ch 3, dc in each of next 3 dc, 2 dc in next dc, (dc in next 4 dc, 2 dc in next dc) around, join (102 dc).

Rnd 9: Beg shell, skip next dc, (shell in next dc, skip next dc) around, join (51 shells).

Rnd 10-14: Sl st in next dc, sl st in next ch sp, beg shell, shell in each shell around, join.

Rnd 15: Sl st in next dc, sl st in next ch sp, ch 3, 4 dc in same sp, sc in next sp between shells, (5 dc in next shell, sc in next sp between shells) around, join, fasten off.

Sleeve Ruffle

Rnd 1: Working around armhole, join with sl st in any ch, ch 3, dc in same ch, dc in each dc and in each ch-1 sp around with 2 dc in each ch, join with sl st in top of ch-3 (28).

Rnd 2: Beg shell, skip next 3 sts, (shell in next st, skip next 2 sts) around, join (9 shells).

Rnd 3: Repeat rnd 10 of Dress.

Rnd 4: Sl st in next dc, sl st in next ch sp, ch 3, 4 dc in same sp, sc in next sp between shells, (5 dc in next shell, sc in next sp between shells) around, join, fasten off. Repeat Sleeve Ruffle in opposite armhole.

Wings

Row 1: For **first side,** ch 16, (dc, ch 1, 2 dc) in 4th ch from hook, (skip next ch, shell in next ch) across, turn (7 shells).

Row 2: Sl st in next dc, sl st in next ch sp, beg shell, shell in each shell across, turn.

Row 3: Sl st in next dc, sl st in next ch sp, beg shell, shell in next 5 shells leaving last shell unworked, turn (6 shells).

Row 4: Ch 1, sl st in first 2 dc, sl st in next ch sp, sl st in next 4 dc, sl st in next ch sp, beg shell, shell in each shell across, turn (5 shells).

Rows 5-7: Repeat rows 3 and 4 alternately, ending with row 3 and 2 shells, fasten off.

Row 1: For **2nd side,** working on opposite side of row 1, with wrong side facing you, join with sl st in first ch, beg shell, (skip next ch, shell in next ch) across, turn (7 shells).

Rows 2-7: Repeat same rows of first side.

Finishing

1: With small paintbrush, paint doll's face as shown in diagram. (Practice painting and blending on scrap of fabric first). Let dry completely. Brush blush onto cheeks.

2: Glue curly hair to head as desired. Tie 10" piece ribbon into a bow, glue to top of head.

3: Apply liquid fabric stiffener to Wings following manufacturer's stiffening instructions. Pin to plastic-covered cardboard. Let dry completely.

4: Place Dress on doll. Cut two pieces ribbon each 27" long. Starting at back, weave one piece through dc of rnd 1. Weave remaining piece through shells on rnd 6. Pull up to fit, tie each ribbon in knot on back leaving ends long. Place Wings on back of Dress by pushing ribbon through corresponding spaces between shells on row 2 of wings. Tie each into a bow.

5: Tie remainder of ribbon into a bow around one dc on center front of row 2. •

FACIAL DIAGRAM

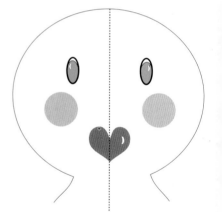

Legend:
- ☒ = Beg Block
- ◆ = End Mesh
- ▨ = Block
- ☐ = Mesh

HEAVENLY ANGELS GRAPH

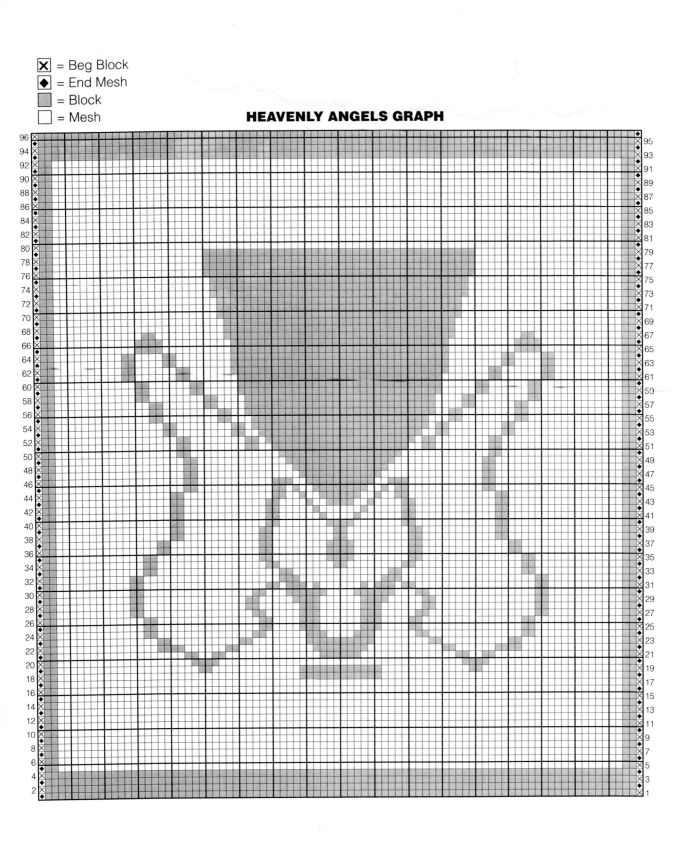

Afghans for the Holidays

Holly Afghan

Designed by Melody MacDuffee

Finished Size

Afghan is 57" x 60".

Materials

○ Worsted-weight yarn — 38 oz. off-white, 8 oz. burgundy and 4 oz. green
○ H crochet hook or size needed to obtain gauge

Gauge

1 slanted shell = 1"; 3 slanted shell rows = 2".

Hollyleaf cluster (make 18)

Rnd 1: For **first leaf,** with green, ch 14, sl st in 2nd ch from hook, (sc in next ch, hdc in next ch, dc in next ch, hdc in next ch, sc in next ch, sl st in next ch) 2 times, ch 2, sl st in same ch as last sl st; working on opposite side of ch, repeat between ( ) 2 times, **do not join.**

Note: For **picot,** ch 3, sl st in top of last st made.

Rnd 2: Working this rnd in **back lps,** picot, *sl st in next 4 sts, picot, sl st in next 6 sts, picot, sl st in each of next 3 sts*, (sl st, ch 3, sl st) in next ch-2 sp; repeat between **; working behind first picot, join with sl st in first sl st.

Rnd 3: For **2nd leaf,** ch 18, sl st in 2nd ch from hook, (sc in next ch, hdc in next ch, dc in next ch, hdc in next ch, sc in next ch, sl st in next ch) 2 times leaving last 4 chs unworked, ch 2, sl st in same ch as last sl st;

working on opposite side of ch, repeat between ( ) 2 times, **do not join.**

Rnd 4: Repeat rnd 2, fasten off.

For **berries,** with wrong side facing you, join burgundy with sl st in picot on one side of ch-4 at center of leaves, *(yo, insert hook in same ch sp, yo, pull up long lp) 5 imes, yo, draw through all lps on hook, ch 1, sl st in same ch sp; repeat from *, fasten off. Repeat in ch-3 sp on opposite side of center ch-4.

Rnd 5: With right side facing you, join off-white with sl st around ch-4 at center of leaves, ch 8, sl st in 2nd st after next set of berries, *ch 8, sl st in 3rd st after next picot, ch 8, sl st in 2nd st after next picot, ch 8, sl st in 2nd st after next ch-3, ch 8, sl st in 3rd st after next picot, ch 8, sl st in 2nd st after next picot*, ch 2, skip both sets of berries, sl st in 2nd st after berries on next leaf; repeat between **, ch 8, join with sl st in first sl st, fasten off (12 ch-8 sps, 1 ch-2 sp).

Afghan

Row 1: With off-white, ch 124, dc in 4th ch from hook, ch 2, sc in same ch, *skip next 2 chs, dc in next ch, (dc, ch 2, sc) in next ch; repeat from * across, turn (31 ch-2 sps).

Note: For **slanted shell,** (2 dc, ch 2, sc) in next ch sp.

Rows 2-71: Ch 2, (dc, ch 2, sc) in first ch sp, slanted shell in each ch-2 sp across, turn (31

slanted shells). At end of last row, **do not turn.**

Rnd 72: Working in ends of rows and sts around outer edge, (ch 5, skip next row, sc in next row) 35 times, ch 7, sc in same row as last sc; working in starting ch on opposite side of row 1, ch 5, skip first 4 chs, sc in next ch, (ch 5, skip next 3 chs, sc in next ch) across, ch 7, sc in same ch as last sc, ch 5, skip first 2 rows, sc in next row, (ch 5, skip next row, sc in next row) 33 times, ch 5, (sc, ch 7, sc) in ch sp of next slanted shell, (ch 5, sc in ch sp of next slanted shell) across, ch 7, sc in same slanted shell as last sc, join with sl st in first ch of first ch-5, fasten off (35 ch-5 sps on each side, 30 ch-5 sps on each end, 1 ch-7 sp at each corner).

Rnd 73: Join burgundy with sl st in any corner ch-7 sp, (ch 2, 2 hdc, picot, 3 hdc) in same sp, 4 hdc in each ch-5 sp around with (3 hdc, picot, 3 hdc) in each corner ch-7 sp, join with sl st in top of ch-2, fasten off (146 hdc on each side, 126 hdc on each end, 4 picots).

Rnd 74: Join off-white with sc in first picot on one long edge, ch 6, sc in same picot, *[ch 4; working in sps between sts, sc in sp between corner hdc group and first 4-hdc group, (ch 4, sc in next sp between 4-hdc groups) across to 4-hdc group before next corner, ch 4, sc in sp between last 4-hdc group

Continued on page 31

Stars & Stripes

Designed by Sandra Miller-Maxfield

Finished Size

Afghan is 48" x 66".

Materials

○ Worsted-weight yarn — 30 oz. white, 14 oz. red and 6 oz. blue
○ 186 each red and blue pony beads
○ Tapestry needle
○ F and H crochet hooks or size needed to obtain gauge

Gauge

With **H hook,** rnds 1-4 of Motif A = 5" across.

Note: Use H hook unless otherwise stated

Motif A (make 21)

Rnd 1: With red, ch 4, sl st in first ch to form ring, ch 1, 12 sc in ring, join with sl st in first sc (12 sc).

Rnd 2: Working this rnd in **back lps** only, ch 4, (dc in next st, ch 1) around, join with sl st in 3rd ch of ch-4 (12 dc, 12 ch-1 sps).

Rnd 3: Ch 1, (sc, ch 2, sc) in same st, 2 sc in next ch-1 sp, sc in next st, 2 sc in next ch-1 sp *(sc, ch 2, sc) in next ch sp, 2 sc in next ch sp, sc in next st, 2 sc in next ch sp; repeat from * around, join with sl st in first sc, fasten off (42 sc, 6 ch-2 sps).

Notes: For **beginning cluster (beg cl),** ch 3, (yo, insert hook in same ch or st, yo, draw lp through, yo, draw through 2 lps

on hook) 4 times, yo, draw through all 5 lps on hook.

For **cluster (cl),** yo, insert hook in next ch or st, yo, draw lp through, yo, draw through 2 lps on hook, (yo, insert hook in same ch or st, yo, draw lp through, yo, draw through 2 lps on hook) 4 times, yo, draw through all 6 lps on hook.

Rnd 4: Join white with sl st in first ch of any ch-2, beg cl, *[ch 3, cl in next ch, ch 1, skip next 3 sts, cl in next st, ch 1, skip next 3 sts], cl in first ch of next ch-2; repeat from * 4 more times; repeat between [ ], join with sl st in top of beg cl, fasten off (18 cls, 12 ch-1 sps, 6 ch-3 sps).

Rnd 5: Join red with sc in any ch-3 sp, ch 2, sc in same sp, sc in top of each cl and in each ch-1 sp around with (sc, ch 2, sc) in each ch-3 sp, join with sl st in first sc, fasten off (42 sc, 6 ch-2 sps).

Rnd 6: Working this rnd in **back lps** only, join white with sl st in first ch of any ch-2, beg cl, *[ch 3, cl in next ch, ch 1, skip next 2 sts, cl in next st, ch 1, skip next st, cl in next st, ch 1, skip next 2 sts], cl in first ch of next ch-2; repeat from * 4 more times; repeat between [ ], join with sl st in top of beg cl, fasten off (24 cls, 18 ch-1 sps, 6 ch-3 sps).

Rnd 7: Join red with sc in any ch-3 sp, (sc, ch 2, sc) in same sp, evenly space 11 sc across to next ch-3 sp, *(2 sc, ch 2, 2 sc) in next ch-3 sp, evenly space 11 sc across to next ch-3 sp;

repeat from * around, join with sl st in first sc, fasten off (90 sc, 6 ch-2 sps).

Motif B (make 21)
Star No. 1

Rnd 1: With white, ch 4, sl st in first ch to form ring, ch 1, 10 sc in ring, join with sl st in first sc (10 sc).

Rnd 2: Ch 3, sc in 2nd ch from hook, hdc in last ch, skip next st; *sl st in next st, ch 3, sc in 2nd ch from hook, hdc in last ch, skip next st; repeat from * around, join with sl st in joining sl st of last rnd, fasten off (5 points).

Stars No. 2-5

Rnd 1: Repeat same rnd of Star No. 1.

Rnd 2: Ch 3, sc in 2nd ch from hook, hdc in last ch, skip next st, *sl st in next st, ch 3, sc in 2nd ch from hook, hdc in last ch, skip next st; repeat from * 2 more times, sl st in next st, ch 2, sl st in corresponding point of last Star (see Joining Diagram on page 18), sc in 2nd ch of ch-2, hdc in first ch of same ch-2, skip next st on this Star, join with sl st in joining sl st of last rnd, fasten off (5 points).

Star No. 6

Rnd 1: Repeat same rnd of Star No. 1.

Rnd 2: Ch 3, sc in 2nd ch from hook, hdc in last ch, skip next st, *sl st in next st, ch 3, sc in

Continued on page 18

Stars & Stripes
Continued from page 16

2nd ch from hook, hdc in last ch, skip next st; repeat from *, sl st in next st, ch 2, sl st in corresponing point of last Star (see diagram), sc in 2nd ch of ch-2, hdc in first ch of same ch-2, skip next st on this Star, sl st in next st, ch 2, sl st in corresponding point of first Star, sc in 2nd ch of ch-2, hdc in first ch of same ch-2, skip next st on this Star, join with sl st in joining sl st of last rnd, fasten off (5 points).

Center
Rnd 1: With blue, ch 4, sl st in first ch to form ring, ch 1, 12 sc in ring, join with sl st in first sc (12 sc).

Rnd 2: Working this rnd in **back lps** only, ch 4, *[sl st over joining sl st between 2 points on Stars, ch 1, dc in next st on rnd 1, ch 1, sl st in next sl st between points, ch 1], dc in next st on rnd 1, ch 1; repeat from * 4 more times; repeat between [ ], join with sl st in 3rd ch of ch-4, fasten off.

Outer Edge
Rnd 1: Working around outer edge of Stars, join blue with sl st in center top point on any Star, *[ch 2, dc in **back lp** of next sl st between points, ch 2, dc next 2 points tog, ch 2, dc in **back lp** of next sl st between points, ch 2], sl st in tip of next point; repeat from * 4 more times; repeat between [ ], join with sl st in first sl st (24 sts, 24 ch-2 sps).

Rnd 2: Ch 1, (sc, ch 2, sc) in first st, *[2 sc in next ch-2 sp, sc in next st, (3 sc in next ch-2 sp, sc in next st) 2 times, 2 sc in next ch-2 sp], (sc ch 2, sc) in next st; repeat from * 4 more times; repeat between [ ], join with sl st in first sc, fas-

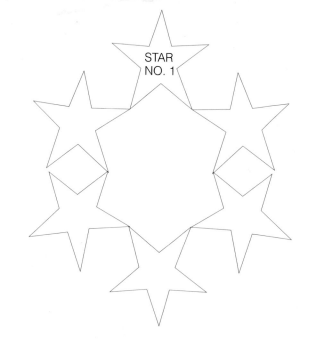

STAR NO. 1

ten off (90 sc, 6 ch-2 sps).

Diamond
Row 1: With white, ch 14, dc in 4th ch from hook, ch 1, skip next ch, (cl in next ch, ch 1, skip next ch) 4 times, dc in last ch, **do not turn,** fasten off (5 ch-1 sps, 4 cls, 3 dc).

Row 2: Join red with sc in top of first ch-3, sc in same st, sc in next dc, (sc in next ch-1 sp, sc in top of next cl) 4 times, sc last ch-1 sp and last dc tog, **do not turn,** fasten off (12 sc).

Row 3: Working this row in **back lps** only, join white with sl st in first st, ch 3, dc in same st, ch 1, skip next st, (cl in next st, ch 1, skip next st) 4 times, dc last 2 sts tog, **do not turn,** fasten off.

Rows 4-5: Repeat rows 2 and 3.

Rnd 6: Working around outer edge, join red with sc in first st, ch 2, sc in same st, *evenly space 13 sc across to last st, (sc, ch 2, sc) in last st, evenly space 13 sc across ends of rows to last row*, (sc, ch 2, sc)

in last row; repeat between **, join with sl st in first sc, fasten off (60 sc, 4 ch-2 sps).

Holding Motifs and Diamonds right sides together, matching sts and ch-2 sps, working through both thicknesses in **front lps** only, with red, sl st together according to Assembly Diagram.

Edging
Notes: With tapestry needle, alternating colors, thread beads onto white, push back until needed.

For **bead picot,** ch 4, sl st in 2nd ch from hook, pull up one bead, skip next ch, sl st in next ch.

Edging is worked in four sections, parts A, B, C and D. When working each section, repeat only instructions from that section unless otherwise stated.

(Part A) Working across top end of Afghan in **back lps,** with F hook and white, join with sl st in first ch of top right-hand corner ch-2 sp (see diagram), bead picot, sl st in next ch, bead picot, [◊*(sl st in each of next 3 sts, bead picot) 4 times, sl st in each of next 3 sts*, sl st in first ch of next ch-2, bead picot, sl st in next ch, bead picot; repeat between **◊, sl st in next ch-2 sp before next seam, bead picot, sl st in next ch sp after seam, bead picot]; repeat between [ ] 4 times; repeat between ◊◊.

(Part B) Working across long edge of Afghan in **back lps,** sl st in first ch of next ch-2, bead picot, sl st in next ch, bead picot; repeat between

[ ] of Part A, ◊*(sl st in each of next 3 sts, bead picot) 4 times, sl st in each of next 3 sts, sl st in first ch of next ch-2, bead picot, sl st in next ch, bead picot*; repeat between **, (sl sl in each of next 3 sts, bead picot) 4 times, sl st in each of next 3 sts, sl st in next ch-2 sp before seam, bead picot, sl st in next ch sp after seam, bead picot◊; repeat between ◊◊ 4 times; repeat between ** 2 times.

(Part C) Working across bottom edge, repeat between [ ] of Part A 5 times; repeat

between ◊◊ of Part A.

(Part D) Working across last long edge, sl st in first ch of next ch-2, bead picot, sl st in next ch, bead picot; repeat between [ ] of Part A; repeat between ◊◊ of Part B 5 times, (sl st in each of next 3 sts, bead picot) 4 times, sl st in each of next 3 sts, sl st in first ch of next ch-2, bead picot, sl st in next ch, bead picot, (sl st in each of next 3 sts, bead picot) 4 times, sl st in each of last 3 sts, join with sl st in first sc, fasten off. •

ASSEMBLY DIAGRAM

Join here for Edging

Afghans for the Holidays

Wonder of Christmas

Designed by Maria Nagy

Finished Size

Afghan is 50" x 65".

Materials

○ Worsted-weight yarn — 18 oz. green, 16 oz. white and 13 oz. red
○ I crochet hook or size needed to obtain gauge

Gauge

3 tr = 1"; 2 tr rows = 2".

Afghan

Row 1: With green, ch 154, tr in 5th ch from hook, tr in next 5 chs, 3 tr in next ch, tr in next 7 chs, (skip next 2 chs, tr in next 7 chs, 3 tr in next ch, tr in next 7 chs) across, turn (153 tr).

Row 2: Ch 4, skip next st, tr in next 6 sts, 3 tr in next st, tr in next 7 sts, (skip next 2 sts, tr in next 7 sts, 3 tr in next st, tr in next 7 sts) 7 times, skip next 2 sts, dc in next 7 sts, 3 dc in next st, dc in next 6 sts, skip next st, dc in last st, turn, fasten off.

Row 3: Join red with sl st in first st, ch 2, skip next st, hdc in next 6 sts, 3 hdc in next st, hdc in next 7 sts, (skip next 2 sts, hdc in next 7 sts, 3 hdc in next st, hdc in next 7 sts) 7 times, skip next 2 sts, hdc in next 7 sts, 3 hdc in next st, hdc in next 6 sts, skip next st, hdc in last st, turn.

Row 4: Ch 2, skip next st, hdc in next 6 sts, 3 hdc in next st, hdc in next 7 sts, (skip next 2 sts, hdc in next 7 sts, 3 hdc in next st, hdc in next 7 sts) 7 times, skip next 2 sts, hdc in next 7 sts, 3 hdc in next st, hdc in next 6 sts, skip next st, hdc in last st, turn, fasten off.

Note: For **puff stitch (puff st),** yo, insert hook in next st, yo, draw up long lp, (yo, insert hook in same st, yo, draw up long lp) 2 times, yo, draw through all 7 lps on hook.

Row 5: Join white with sl st in first st, ch 1, puff st in same st, (ch 1, skip next st, puff st in next st) 3 times, *[(ch 1, puff st in next st) 4 times, (ch 1, skip next st, puff st in next st) 2 times], ch 1, skip next 4 sts, puff st in next st, (ch 1, skip next st, puff st in next st) 2 times; repeat from * across to last 10 sts, (ch 1, puff st in next st) 4 times, (ch 1, skip next st, puff st in next st) 3 times, turn (82 ch-1 sps).

Row 6: Sl st in first ch-1 sp, ch 1, puff st in same sp, ch 1, skip next ch-1 sp, (puff st in next ch-1 sp, ch 1) 3 times, puff st in top of next puff st, *(ch 1, puff st in next ch-1 sp) 4 times, ch 1, skip next ch-1 sp, (puff st in next ch-1 sp, ch 1) 4 times, puff st in top of next puff st; repeat from * across to last 5 ch-1 sps, (ch 1, puff st in next ch-1 sp) 3 times, ch 1, skip next ch-1 sp, puff st in last ch-1 sp, turn, fasten off (81 puff sts, 80 ch-1 sps).

Row 7: Join green with sl st in first st, ch 4, skip next ch-1 sp, tr in next 6 sts and ch-1 sps, 3 tr in next st, *tr in next 7 ch-1 sps and sts, skip next 2 sts and one ch-1 sp, tr in next 7 sts and ch-1 sps, 3 tr in next st; repeat from * across to last 8 ch-1 sps and sts, tr in next 6 ch-1 sps and sts, skip next ch-1 sp, tr in last st, turn (153 tr).

Rows 8-12: Repeat rows 2-6.

Row 13: Join red with sl st in first st, ch 2, skip next ch-1 sp, hdc in next 6 sts and ch-1 sps, 3 hdc in next st, *hdc in next 7 ch-1 sps and sts, skip next 2 sts and one ch-1 sp, hdc in next 7 sts and ch-1 sps, 3 hdc in next st; repeat from * across to last 8 ch-1 sps and sts, hdc in next 6 ch-1 sps and sts, skip next ch-1 sp, hdc in last st, turn (153 hdc).

Row 14: Repeat row 4.

Row 15: Join green with sl st in first st, ch 4, skip next st, tr in next 6 sts, 3 tr in next st, tr in next 7 sts, (skip next 2 sts, tr in next 7 sts, 3 tr in next st, tr in next 7 sts) 7 times, skip next 2 sts, dc in next 7 sts, 3 dc in next st, dc in next 6 sts, skip next st, dc in last st, turn.

Row 16: Repeat row 2.

Rows 17-18: Repeat rows 5 and 6.

Rows 19-20: Repeat rows 13 and 4.

Row 21: Repeat row 15.

Rows 22-82: Repeat rows 2-21 consecutively, ending with row 2. At end of last row, fasten off. •

Patriotic Pinwheel

Designed by Jocelyn Sass

Finished Size

Afghan is 49" x 65".

Materials

○ Chunky yarn — 46 oz. white, 25 oz. blue and 21 oz. red
○ Tapestry needle
○ I crochet hook or size needed to obtain gauge

Gauge

3 sc = 1"; 3 sc rows = 1". Each Block is 16" square.

Block (make 12)

Note: When changing colors (see page 158), always drop yarn to wrong side of work. Use a separate skein of yarn for each color section. **Do not** carry yarn across from one section to another. Fasten off at end of each color section.

Front of row 2 is right side of work.

Work odd-numbered rows on graph from left to right and even-numbered rows from right to left.

Each square on graph equals one sc.

Row 1: With white, ch 45, sc in 2nd ch from hook, sc in each ch across, turn (44 sc)

Row 2: For **row 2 of graph,** ch 1, sc in first 11 sts changing to blue in last st made, sc in next st changing to white, sc in next 20 sts changing to blue in last st made, sc in next st changing to white, sc in last 11 sts, turn.

Rows 3-44: Ch 1, sc in each st across changing colors according to graph, turn.

Rnd 45: Working in rnds, ch 1, 3 sc in first st, sc in each st and in end of each row around with 3 sc in each corner st, join with sl st in first sc, fasten off.

Rnd 46: Join red with sc in any st, sc in each st around with 2 sc in each center corner st, join, fasten off.

Holding Blocks wrong sides together, matching sts, with red, sew together through **back lps** in 3 rows of 4 Blocks each.

For **edging,** working around entire outer edge, join red with sl st in first st of any 2-sc group on any corner, ch 2, 2 hdc in same st, 2 hdc in next st, (hdc in each st across to one st before next corner 2-sc group, 2 hdc in next st, 3 hdc in next st, 2 hdc in next st) 3 times, hdc in each st across with 2 hdc in last st, join with sl st in top of ch-2, fasten off. •

☐ = White
▨ = Blue
■ = Red

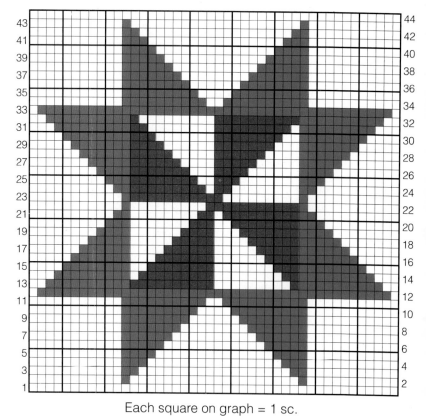

Each square on graph = 1 sc.

Cross Afghan

Designed by Hazel Osburn Jones

Finished Size

Afghan is 49½" x 72".

Materials

○ Worsted-weight yarn — 35 oz. burgundy (MC) and 27 oz. soft white (CC)
○ H crochet hook or size needed to obtain gauge

Gauge

3 brick sts = 4"; 3 brick st rows = 2".

Afghan

Row 1: With MC, ch 149, 3 dc in 5th ch from hook, skip next 3 chs, *(sc, ch 3, 3 dc) in next ch, skip next 3 chs; repeat from * across to last ch, sc in last ch, turn (35 ch-3 sps).

Notes: For **beginning brick st (beg brick st),** ch 4, 3 dc in same sc.

For brick st, (sc, ch 3, 3 dc) in next ch-3 sp.

Rows 2-12: Beg brick st, brick st across to last ch-4, sc in last ch-4 sp, turn (36 brick sts, 1 sc).

Note: When changing colors (see page 158), always drop color to wrong side of work. Do not carry yarn across from one section to another. Use a separate skein or ball of yarn for each color section.

Rows 13-22: Beg brick st, brick st 5 times changing to CC in last st made, brick st 25 times changing to MC in last st made, brick st 5 times, sc in last ch-4 sp, turn.

Rows 23-61: Beg brick st, brick st 5 times changing to CC in last st made, brick st 10 times changing to MC in last st made, brick st 5 times changing to CC in last st made, brick st 10 times changing to MC in last st made, brick st 5 times, sc in last ch-4 sp, turn.

Rows 62-69: Beg brick st, brick st 5 times changing to CC in last st made, brick st 5 times changing to MC in last st made, brick st 15 times changing to CC in last st made, brick st 5 times changing to MC in last st made, brick st 5 times, sc in last ch-4 sp, turn.

Rows 70-81: Repeat row 23.

Rows 82-91: Repeat row 13. At end of last row, fasten off CC.

Rows 92-106: Repeat row 2. At end of last row, **do not fasten off.**

Edging

Working around outer edge, beg brick st, brick st across to last ch-4 sp, sc in ch-4 sp; working in ends of rows down side, beg brick st in last sc made, (skip next row, brick st in sc at end of next row) across; working in starting ch on opposite side of row 1, brick st in first ch-3 sp, brick st in next ch, (skip next ch-3 sp, brick st in next ch) across; working in ends of rows up side, skip first row, (brick st in sc at end of next row, skip next row) across to last row, sl st in last row, fasten off. •

Giving Thanks

Designed by Sandra Miller-Maxfield

Finished Size

Afghan is 55½" x 67½".

Materials

- ○ Worsted-weight yarn — 18 oz. each camel, brown and variegated, 15 oz. each rust and gold, 6 oz. green
- ○ G crochet hook or size needed to obtain gauge

Gauge

Rnds 1 and 2 of Motif = 3¼" across. Each Motif is 6" square.

First Row
First Motif

Notes: For **beginning double crochet popcorn (beg dc pc),** ch 3, 4 dc in ring, drop lp from hook, insert hook in top of ch-3, draw dropped lp through.

For **double crochet popcorn (dc pc),** 5 dc in ring, drop lp from hook, insert hook in first dc of 5-dc group, draw dropped lp through.

Rnd 1: With rust, ch 6, sl st in first ch to form ring, beg pc, ch 3, (pc, ch 3) 7 times, join with sl st in top of beg pc, fasten off (8 pc, 8 ch-3 sps).

Note: For **cluster (cl),** (yo, insert hook in last sc made, yo, draw lp through, yo, draw through 2 lps on hook) 3 times, yo, draw through all 4 lps on hook.

Rnd 2: Join green with sc in any ch sp, ch 4, cl, (sc in next ch sp, ch 4, cl) around, join with sl st in first sc, fasten off (8 cls).

Note: For **treble popcorn (tr pc),** 5 tr in next sp, drop lp from hook, insert hook in first tr of 5-tr group, draw dropped lp through.

Rnd 3: Join gold with sl st in sp between any 2 cls, ch 3, 2 dc in same sp, ch 1, (tr pc, ch 3, tr pc, ch 3, tr pc) in sp between next 2 cls, ch 1, *3 dc in sp between next 2 cls, ch 1, (tr pc, ch 3, tr pc, ch 3, tr pc) in sp between next 2 cls, ch 1; repeat from * around, join with sl st in top of ch-3, fasten off.

Rnd 4: Join variegated with sl st in any corner tr pc, ch 3, (dc, ch 1, 2 dc) in same st, *[3 dc in next ch-3 sp, 3 dc in each of next 2 ch-1 sps, 3 dc in next ch-3 sp], (2 dc, ch 1, 2 dc) in next tr pc; repeat from * 2 more times; repeat between [ ], join, fasten off.

Rnd 5: Join camel with sl st in any corner ch sp, ch 3, (2 dc, ch 1, 3 dc) in same sp, *[3 dc in sp between next 2-dc group and next 3-dc group, (3 dc in sp between next 2 3-dc groups) 3 times, 3 dc in sp between next 3-dc group and next 2-dc group], (3 dc, ch 1, 3 dc) in next corner ch sp; repeat from * 2 more times; repeat between [ ], join, fasten off.

Rnd 6: Join brown with sc in any corner ch sp, ch 3, sc in same sp, *[ch 3, (sc in sp between next 2 3-dc groups, ch 3) 6 times], (sc, ch 3, sc) in next corner ch sp; repeat from * 2 more times; repeat between [ ], join with sl st in first sc, fasten off.

Second Motif

Rnds 1-5: Reversing gold and rust, repeat same rnds of First Motif.

Rnd 6: Join brown with sc in any corner ch sp; joining to side of last Motif, ch 1, sc in corresponding corner ch sp on other Motif, ch 1, sc in same sp on this Motif, ch 1, sc in next ch sp on other Motif, ch 1, (sc in sp between next 2 3-dc groups on this Motif, ch 1, sc in next ch sp on other Motif, ch 1) 6 times, sc in next corner ch sp on this Motif, ch 1, sc in next corner ch sp on other Motif, ch 1, sc in same sp on this Motif, *[ch 3, (sc in sp between next 2 3-dc groups, ch 3) 6 times], (sc, ch 3, sc) in next corner ch sp; repeat from *; repeat between [ ], join with sl st in first sc, fasten off.

Third Motif

Rnds 1-5: Repeat same rnds of First Motif.

Rnd 6: Repeat same rnd of Second Motif.

Repeat Second and Third Motifs alternately for a total of 9 Motifs.

Continued on page 30

Spring Medley

Designed by Sandra Miller-Maxfield

Finished Size

Afghan is 47" x 65".

Materials

○ Worsted-weight yarn — 26 oz. med. green, 13 oz. lt. green, 11 oz. white, 3 oz. each blue, yellow, lilac and pink
○ Tapestry needle
○ G crochet hook or size needed to obtain gauge

Gauge

Rnds 1-3 of Block = 3" across; 4 sc = 1". Each Block is 6" square.

Block (make 70)

Notes: For **beginning cluster (beg cl),** ch 3, (yo, insert hook in same sp, yo, draw lp through, yo, draw through 2 lps on hook) 3 times, yo, draw through all 4 lps on hook.

For **cluster (cl),** yo, insert hook in next ch sp, yo, draw lp through, yo, draw through 2 lps on hook, (yo, insert hook in same sp, yo, draw lp through, yo, draw through 2 lps on hook) 3 times, yo, draw through all 5 lps on hook.

Rnds 1-3 form a flower motif in each Block. Make 18 blue, 18 pink, 17 lilac and 17 yellow. Work remainder of Bock using colors indicated.

Rnd 1: With flower color, ch 4, sl st in first ch to form ring, ch 1, (sc in ring, ch 1) 8 times, join with sl st in first sc (8 sc, 8 ch sps).

Rnd 2: Sl st in first ch sp, ch 3, (sl st in next ch sp, ch 3) around, join with sl st in first sl st.

Rnd 3: Sl st in first ch sp, beg cl, ch 4, (cl in next ch sp, ch 4) around, join with sl st in top of beg cl, fasten off (8 cls, 8 ch-4 sps).

Rnd 4: Join white with sc in any ch-4 sp, (sc, ch 3, 2 sc) in same sp, ch 1, *(2 sc, ch 3, 2 sc) in next ch-4 sp, ch 1; repeat from * around, join with sl st in first sc (8 ch-3 sps, 8 ch-1 sps).

Rnd 5: Sl st in next st, sl st in next ch sp, ch 1, (sc, ch 3, sc) in same sp, ch 3, sl st in next ch-1 sp, ch 3, *(sc, ch 3, sc) in next ch-3 sp, ch 3, sl st in next ch-1 sp, ch 3; repeat from * around, join, fasten off (24 ch-3 sps).

Rnd 6: Join med. green with sl st in first ch-3 sp, (ch 3, dc, ch 3, 2 dc) in same sp, ch 2, dc in each of next 2 ch-3 sps, ch 2, sc in next ch-3 sp, ch 2, dc in each of next 2 ch-3 sps, ch 2, *(2 dc, ch 3, 2 dc) in next ch-3 sp, ch 2, dc in each of next 2 ch-3 sps, ch 2, sc in

Continued on page 30

Spring Medley

Continued from page 28

next ch-3 sp, ch 2, dc in each of next 2 ch-3 sps, ch 2; repeat from * around, join with sl st in top of ch-3 (32 dc, 16 ch-2 sps, 4 sc, 4 ch-3 sps).

Rnd 7: Ch 1, sc in each st and 2 sc in each ch-2 sp around with (2 sc, ch 2, 2 sc) in each ch-3 sp, join with sl st in first sc, fasten off (84 sc, 4 ch-2 sps).

Rnd 8: Join lt. green with sc in any ch-2 sp, ch 3, sc in same sp, ch 1, skip next st, (sc in next st, ch 1, skip next st) around to next ch-2 sp, *(sc, ch 3, sc) in next ch-2 sp, ch 1, skip next st, (sc in next st, ch 1, skip next st) around to next ch-2 sp; repeat from * around, join, fasten off (48 sc, 44 ch-1 sps, 4 ch-3 sps).

Arrange Blocks in desired color pattern and sew together through **back lps** in seven rows of ten Blocks each.

Border

Rnd 1: Working around entire outer edge, with right side facing you, join lt. green with sc in any corner ch-3 sp, ch 3, sc in same sp, sc in each st, sc in each ch-1 sp, hdc in each ch sp on each side of seams and hdc in each seam around with (sc, ch-3, sc) in each corner ch-3 sp, join with sl st in first sc (181 sc across each short end between corner ch sps, 259 sc across each long edge between corner ch sps).

Rnd 2: Sl st in first corner ch sp, ch 1, (sc, ch 3, sc) in same sp, *[ch 1, skip next st, (sc in next st, ch 1, skip next st) across] to next corner ch sp, (sc, ch 3, sc) in next ch sp; repeat from * 2 more times, repeat between [ ], join, fasten off.

Rnd 3: Join med. green with sl st in any corner ch sp, (ch 3, dc, ch 2, 2 dc) in same sp, *[ch 1, (sc in next ch-1 sp, ch 1) across] to next corner ch sp, (2 dc, ch 2, 2 dc) in next ch sp; repeat from * 2 more times; repeat between [ ], join with sl st in top of ch-3.

Rnd 4: Ch 1, sc in each st and in each ch-1 sp around with (sc, ch 3, sc) in each corner ch-2 sp, join with sl st in first sc.

Note: For **shell,** (2 dc, ch 2, 2 dc) in next st.

Rnd 5: Sl st in next st, ch 1, sc in same st, skip next st, (3 dc, ch 2, 3 dc) in next ch sp, *skip next st, sc in next st, (skip next 2 sts, shell in next st, skip next 2 sts, sc in next st) around to last sc before next ch-3 sp, skip next st, (3 dc, ch 2, 3 dc) in next ch sp; repeat from * 2 more times, skip next st, (sc in next st, skip next 2 sts, shell in next st, skip next 2 sts) around, join with sl st in first sc.

Rnd 6: Ch 2, skip next dc, sl st in next dc, ch 2, skip next dc, (sl st, ch 3, sl st, ch 3, sl st) in next ch-2 sp, ◊ch 2, skip next dc, sl st in next dc, ch 2, skip next dc, sl st in next dc, *ch 2, (sl st, ch 2, sl st) in ch sp of next shell, ch 2, sl st in next sc; repeat from * around to next corner, ch 2, skip next dc, sl st in next dc, ch 2, skip next dc, (sl st, ch 3, sl st, ch 3, sl st) in next ch-2 sp; repeat from ◊ 2 more times, ch 2, skip next dc, sl st in next dc, ch 2, skip next dc, [sl st in next sc, ch 2, (sl st, ch 2, sl st) in ch sp of next shell, ch 2]; repeat between [ ] around, join with sl st in joining sl st of last rnd, fasten off. •

Giving Thanks

Continued from page 27

Second Row
First Motif

Joining to bottom of First Motif on last row, work same as First Row Second Motif.

Second Motif

Rnds 1-5: Repeat same rnds of First Row First Motif.

Rnd 6: Join brown with sc in any corner ch sp; joining to bottom of next Motif on last row, ch 1, sc in corresponding corner ch sp on other Motif, ch 1, sc in same sp on this Motif, *ch 1, sc in next ch sp on other Motif, ch 1, (sc in sp between next 2 3-dc groups on this Motif, ch 1, sc in next ch sp on other Motif, ch 1) 6 times, sc in next corner ch sp on this Motif, ch 1, sc in next corner ch sp on other Motif, ch 1, sc in same sp on this Motif*; joining to side of last Motif on this row; repeat between **, [ch 3, (sc in sp between next 2 3-dc groups, ch 3) 6 times], (sc, ch 3, sc) in next corner ch sp; repeat between [ ], join with sl st in first sc, fasten off.

Third Motif

Rnds 1-5: Reversing gold and rust, repeat same rnds of First Row First Motif.

Rnd 6: Repeat same rnd of Second Row Second Motif.

Repeat Second and Third Motifs alternately for a total of 9 Motifs.

Third Row
First Motif
Joining to bottom of First Motif on last row, work same as First Row Third Motif.

Second Motif
Rnds 1-5: Reversing gold and rust, repeat same rnds of First Row First Motif on page 27.
Rnd 6: Repeat same rnd of Second Row Second Motif.

Third Motif
Rnds 1-5: Repeat same rnds of First Row First Motif.
Rnd 6: Repeat same rnd of Second Row Second Motif.
Repeat Second and Third Motifs alternately for a total of 9 Motifs.
Repeat Second and Third

Rows alternately for a total of 11 Rows.

Edging
Rnd 1: Working around entire outer edge, join brown with sc in any corner ch sp, ch 3, sc in same sp, ch 3, (sc in next ch sp, ch 3) across to next corner ch sp, *(sc, ch 3, sc) in next corner ch sp, ch 3, (sc in next ch sp, ch 3) across to next corner ch sp; repeat from * around, join with sl st in first sc.
Rnd 2: Sl st in first ch sp, ch 3, 8 dc in same sp, (*skip next sc, 3 dc in each sc across to sc before next corner ch sp, skip next sc*, 9 dc in next corner ch sp) 3 times; repeat between **, join with sl st in top of ch-3.
Notes: For **beginning front post cluster (beg fp cl),** ch 3, *yo, insert hook from front to back around post of next st, yo,

draw lp through, yo, draw through 2 lps on hook; repeat from *, yo, draw through all 3 lps on hook.

For **front post cluster (fp cl),** (yo, insert hook from front to back around post of next st, yo, draw lp through, yo, draw through 2 lps on hook) 3 times, yo, draw through all 4 lps on hook.
Rnd 3: Beg fp cl; *[(working behind last rnd, dc in corner ch sp on rnd before last, fp cl on last rnd) 2 times; working behind last rnd, dc in next ch sp on rnd before last, (fp cl on last rnd; working behind last rnd, dc in next ch sp on rnd before last) across] to next corner 9-dc group, fp cl; repeat from * 2 more times; repeat between [ ], join with sl st in top of beg fp cl, fasten off. •

Holly Afghan
Continued from page 15

and corner hdc group, ch 4], (sc, ch 6, sc) in next picot; repeat from * 2 more times; repeat between [ ], join with sl st in first sc.
Rnd 75: Sl st in each of first 2 chs of next ch-6, ch 1, (sc, ch 4, sc) in same sp, *(ch 4, sc in next ch sp) across to next corner ch sp, ch 4, (sc, ch 4, sc) in next corner ch sp; repeat from * 2 more times, (ch 4, sc in next ch sp) across, ch 4, join.
Rnd 76: Sl st in each of first 2 chs of next ch-4, ch 1, sc in same ch sp, ch 4, (sc in next ch sp, ch 4) around, join (146 ch sps).
Rnd 77: Ch 1, 4 hdc in first st, 4 hdc in each ch-4 sp around with 4 hdc in each corner sc, join with sl st in first hdc (600 hdc).
Rnd 78: Ch 1, sc in next st, (ch

6, skip next 5 sts, sc in next st, ch 6, skip next 4 sts, sc in next st, ch 3, sl st in ch-8 sp below first set of berries on one Leaf Cluster, ch 3, skip next 4 sts on Afghan, sc in next st, ch 3, sl st in next ch-8 sp on Leaf Cluster, ch 3, skip next 4 sts on Afghan, sc in next st, ch 6, skip next 4 sts, sc in next st, ch 6, skip next 5 sts, sc in next st) 5 times, [ch 6, skip next 5 sts, sc in next st, ch 6, skip next 5 sts, sc in next st, ch 3, sl st in ch-8 sp below first set of berries on one Leaf Cluster, ch 3, skip next 4 sts on Afghan, sc in next st, ch 3, sl st in next ch-8 sp on Leaf Cluster, ch 3, skip next 4 sts on Afghan, sc in next st, ch 6, skip next 5 sts, sc in next st, ch 6, skip next 5 sts, sc in next st], *ch 6, skip next 5 sts, sc in next st, ch 6, skip next 5 sts, sc in next st, ch 3, sl

st in ch-8 sp below first set of berries on one Leaf Cluster, ch 3, skip next 5 sts on Afghan, sc in next st, ch 3, sl st in next ch-8 sp on Leaf Cluster, ch 3, skip next 5 sts on Afghan, sc in next st, ch 6, skip next 5 sts, sc in next st, ch 6, skip next 5 sts, sc in next st*; repeat between **; repeat between [ ]; repeat between ( ) 5 times; repeat between [ ]; repeat between ** 2 times; repeat between [ ] omitting last sc, join wth sl st in first sc.
Rnd 79: Sl st in next 3 chs of first ch-6, ch 1, sc in same ch sp, ch 6, sc in next ch sp; working around Leaf Cluster, *[ch 3, sl st in next free ch sp on Leaf Cluster, (ch 8, sl st in next ch sp) 2 times, ch 8, sl st in same ch sp as last sl st, (ch 8, sl st in

Continued on page 32

Holly Afghan

Continued from page 31

next ch sp) 2 times, ch 4, skip next ch-2 sp, sl st in next ch sp, (ch 8, sl st in next ch sp) 2 times, ch 8, sl st in same ch sp as last sl st, (ch 8, sl in next ch sp) 2 times, ch 3, sc in next ch sp on last rnd of Afghan], (ch 6, sc in next ch sp) 3 times; repeat from * 16 more times; repeat between [ ], ch 6, sc in next ch sp, ch 6, join.

Rnd 80: Sl st in each of first 2 chs of next ch-6, ch 1, sc in same sp, ◊*[ch 3, skip next ch-3 sp, sl st in next ch-8 sp, (ch 8, sl st in next ch sp) 10 times, ch 3, skip next ch-3 sp, sc in next ch-6 sp], (ch 6, sc in next ch sp) 2 times*; repeat between ** 3 more times; repeat between [ ]; for **corner,** ch 6, (sc, ch 8, sc) in next ch sp, ch 6, sc in next ch sp; repeat between ** 3 more times; repeat between [ ]◊, corner; repeat between ◊◊, ch 6, (sc, ch 3, sc) in next ch sp, ch 6, join, fasten off.

Rnd 81: Join off-white with sc in corner ch sp before one long edge, ch 6, sc in next ch sp, •◊ch 2, skip next ch-3 sp, sl st in next ch 8 sp, (ch 8, sl st in next ch sp) 3 times, ch 8, dc in next ch sp, ch 4, dc in next ch sp, (ch 8, sl st in next ch sp) 4 times, ch 2, skip next ch-3 sp, dc in next ch sp, ch 4, dc in next ch sp◊, *[ch 2, skip next ch-3 sp, sl st in next ch-8 sp; to **join,** ch 3, sl st back into last ch-8 sp made on this rnd, ch 5, sl st in next ch sp on last rnd, ch 3, sl st back into next to the last ch-8 sp made on this rnd, ch 5, sl st in next ch sp on last rnd; ch 8, sl st in next ch sp, ch 8, dc in next ch sp, ch 4, dc in

next ch sp, (ch 8, sl st in next ch sp) 4 times], ch 2, skip next ch-3 sp, dc in next ch sp, ch 4, dc in next ch sp*; repeat between ** 2 more times; repeat between [ ], ch 3, skip next ch-3 sp, sl st in next ch sp, (ch 6, sc in next ch sp) 2 times; repeat between ◊◊; repeat between ** 2 more times; repeat between [ ], ch 3, skip next ch-3 sp, sl st in next ch sp•, (ch 6, sc in next ch sp) 2 times; repeat between ••, ch 6, sc in last ch sp, ch 6, join.

Rnd 82: Sl st in each of first 2 chs of next ch-6, ch 1, 2 hdc in same ch sp, hdc in next ch-2 sp, 6 hdc in next ch sp, 10 hdc in next ch sp, ◊(6 hdc in each of next 5 ch sps, 2 hdc in each of next 2 ch sps) 4 times, 6 hdc in each of next 5 ch sps, [10 hdc in next ch sp, 6 hdc in next ch sp, hdc in next ch sp, 2 hdc in each of next 2 ch sps, hdc in next ch sp, 6 hdc in next ch sp, 10 hdc in next ch sp]; repeat between ( ) 3 times, 6 hdc in each of next 5 ch sps◊; repeat between [ ]; repeat between ◊◊, 10 hdc in next ch sp, 6 hdc in next ch sp, hdc in next ch sp, 2 hdc in last ch sp, join with sl st in top of first hdc.

Rnd 83: Ch 1, sc in first st, ch 4, skip next 4 sts, sc in next st, ch 4, skip next 3 sts, sc in next st, *(ch 4, skip next st, sc in next st) 5 times, (ch 4, skip next 3 sts, sc in next st) 41 times, (ch 4, skip next 2 sts, sc in next st, ch 4, skip next st, sc in next st) 2 times, ch 4, skip next st, sc in next st, ch 4, skip next 3 sts, sc in next st, (ch 4, skip next 4 sts, sc in next st) 2 times, ch 4, skip next 3 sts, sc in next st, (ch 4, skip next st, sc in next st) 5 times, (ch 4, skip next 3 sts, sc in next st) 33 times, (ch 4, skip

next st, sc in next st) 5 times, ch 4, skip next 3 sts, sc in next st*, (ch 4, skip next 4 sts, sc in next st) 2 times, ch 4, skip next 3 sts, sc in next st; repeat between **, ch 4, skip last 4 sts, join with sl st in first sc.

Rnd 84: Sl st in each of first 2 chs of next ch-4, ch 1, sc in same ch sp, ch 4, (sc in next ch sp, ch 4) around, join.

Rnd 85: Sl st in each of first 2 chs of next ch-4, ch 1 sc in same ch sp, ch 4, (sc in next ch sp, ch 4) around skipping each center corner ch sp, join, fasten off.

Rnd 86: Join burgundy with sl st in any ch sp, ch 1, 4 hdc in same sp, 4 hdc in each ch sp around skipping each center corner ch sp, join with sl st in first hdc, fasten off.

Rnd 87: Join off white with sc between 4-hdc groups above skipped corner ch sp before one short end of Afghan, ch 4; working in spaces between 4-hdc groups, (sc in next sp, ch 4) around, join.

Rnd 88: (Sl st, ch 1, sc) in next ch sp, *[ch 4, (sc, ch 5, sc) in next ch sp, ch 4, sc in next ch sp*; repeat between ** 3 more times, (ch 4, sc in next ch sp) 28 times; repeat between ** 4 more times, sc in next ch sp; repeat between ** 4 more times, (ch 4, sc in next ch sp) 36 times; repeat between ** 4 more times], sc in next ch sp; repeat between [ ], join.

Rnd 89: Sl st in each of first 2 chs of next ch-4, ch 1, sc in same ch sp, ch 4, (sc in next ch sp, ch 4) around, join.

Rnd 90: Sl st in next ch sp, ch 1, 4 hdc in each ch sp around skipping each center corner ch sp, join with sl st in first hdc, fasten off. •

Christmas Superstitions from Around the World

It was believed that midwinter is a time when spirits and monsters were on the prowl. It is also a time to look forward to the coming of spring which made it a good time for fortune telling and weather forecasting.

At midnight on Christmas Eve, all water turns to wine; cattle kneel facing the East; horses kneel and blow as if to warm the manger; animals can speak, though it's bad luck to hear them; bees hum the hundredth psalm.

In Ireland, it is believed that the gates of heaven open at midnight on Christmas Eve. Those who die at that time go straight to heaven without having to wait in purgatory.

A child born on Christmas Day or Christmas Eve is considered very lucky in some countries, but in Greece he is feared to be a Kallikantzaroi; in Poland he may turn out to be a werewolf.

The weather on each of the twelve days of Christmas signifies what the weather will be on the appropriate month of the coming year.

In Germany, the first girl in a circle that gets touched by a blindfolded goose will wed first.

The branch of a cherry tree placed in water at the beginning of Advent will bring luck if it flowers by Christmas.

In Devonshire, England, if a rooster crows when a girl speaks at the hen house door on Christmas Eve, she will marry within the year.

You burn your old shoes during the Christmas season in Greece to prevent misfortunes in the coming year.

It's bad luck to let any fire go out in your house during the Christmas season.

If the husband brings the Christmas holly into the house first, he will rule the household for the coming year.

If you eat a raw egg before eating anything else on Christmas morning, you will be able to carry weights.

In Hertfordshire, England, a good harvest is determined by sticking a plum cake on a cow's horn and throwing cider into its face on Christmas Eve. If the cake falls forward, there will be a good harvest.

From cockcrow to daybreak of Christmas morning, stay indoors while the trolls roam the Swedish countryside.

Buried treasure reveals itself during the recitation of Christ's genealogy at midnight during Mass on Christmas.

If you don't eat any plum pudding, you will lose a friend before the next Christmas.

You will have bad luck for a year if you refuse mince pie at Christmas dinner.

A loaf of bread left on the table after Christmas Eve dinner will ensure no lack of bread for the next year.

Eating an apple at midnight on Christmas Eve gives good health for a year.

It's bad luck to let your evergreen decorations fall or to throw them away. You should burn them or feed them to your cow.

Chapter Two

Gifts for the Holidays

It's difficult to decide just who derives the most fun from a gift, the giver or the receiver. There's the combined pleasure of one's love of needlework added to the excitement and appreciation expressed by the recipient of a homemade gift. Each stitch is made with that one person in mind. It speaks straight from one heart to another.

Christmas Place Mat Set

Designed by Zelda Workman

Finished Size

Place Mat is 13" x 17".
Coaster is 5" square.

Materials

○ Size 10 bedspread cotton —
   250 yds. green/red/white
   multicolor, 75 yds. white
○ No. 7 steel crochet hook or
   size needed to obtain gauge

Gauge

Each Motif measures 2" across.
Note: This project may ruffle
   until blocked.

PLACE MAT

Block (make 12)
First Motif
Rnd 1: With white, ch 4, sl st
   in first ch to form ring, ch 1,
   (sc, ch 11, sc, ch 13) 4 times
   in ring, join with sl st in first
   sc, fasten off (4 ch-13 lps,
   4 ch-11 lps).
Note: For **cluster (cl),** yo, insert
   hook in next ch sp, yo, draw
   lp through, yo, draw through
   2 lps on hook, (yo, insert hook
   in same sp, yo, draw lp
   through, yo, draw 2 lps on
   hook) 2 times, yo, draw
   through all 4 lps on hook.
Rnd 2: Join multicolor with sc in
   any ch-11 lp, ch 4, (cl, ch 4,
   cl, ch 4, cl) in next ch-13 lp,
   ch 4, *sc in next ch-11 lp, ch

4, (cl, ch 4, cl, ch 4, cl) in
next ch-13 lp, ch 4; repeat
from * around, join, fasten off
(16 ch-4 sps).

1-Side Joined Motif
Rnd 1: Repeat same rnd of
   First Motif.
Rnd 2: Join multicolor with sc in
   any ch-11 lp, ch 4, (cl, ch 4,
   cl) in next ch-13 lp; working
   on side of First Motif (see
   Motif Joining Diagram on
   page 38), ch 2, sl st in corresponding ch-4 sp on First
   Motif, ch 2, cl in same ch lp
   on this Motif, ch 2, sl st in
   next ch-4 sp on other Motif, ch
   2, sc in next ch-11 lp on this
   Motif, ch 2, sl st in next ch-4
   sp on other Motif, ch 2, cl in
   next ch-13 lp on this Motif, ch
   2, sl st in next ch-4 sp on
   other Motif, ch 2, (cl, ch 4, cl)
   in same ch lp on this Motif
   *ch 4, sc in next ch-11 lp, ch
   4, (cl, ch 4, cl, ch 4, cl) in
   next ch-13 lp; repeat from *,
   ch 4, join, fasten off.
Joining to bottom of First Motif,
work 1-Side Joined Motif.

2-Side Joined Motif
Rnd 1: Work same rnd of First
   Motif.
Rnd 2: Join multicolor with sc in
   any ch-11 lp, ch 4, (cl, ch 4,
   cl) in next ch-13 lp; working
   on bottom of Second Motif on
   row above, ch 2, sl st in corresponding ch-4 sp on other

Motif, ch 2, cl in same ch lp
on this Motif, *ch 2, sl st in
next ch-4 sp on other Motif, ch
2, sc in next ch-11 lp on this
Motif, ch 2, sl st in next ch-4
sp on other Motif, ch 2, cl in
next ch-13 lp on this Motif, ch
2, sl st in next ch-4 sp on other
Motif, ch 2*, cl in same ch lp
on this Motif; working on side
of last Motif on this row, ch 2,
sl st in next ch-4 sp on other
Motif, ch 2, cl in same ch lp
on this Motif; repeat between
**, (cl, ch 4, cl) in same ch lp
on this Motif, ch 4, sc in next
ch-11 lp, ch 4, (cl, ch 4, cl, ch
4, cl) in next ch-13 lp, ch 4,
join, fasten off.

First Row
First Block
Working around outer edge of one
   Block, join white with sc in
   upper right corner ch-4 sp (see
   Motif Joining Diagram on page
   38), ch 4, (sc in next ch sp or
   joining, ch 4) around, join with
   sl st in first sc, fasten off.

Second Block
Join white with sc in upper right
   corner ch-4 sp, (ch 4, sc in
   next ch sp or joining) 9 times;
   working on side of last Block
   (see Block Joining Diagram),
   (ch 2, sc in corresponding ch-
   4 sp on last Block, ch 2, sc in
   next ch-4 sp on this Block) 3

Continued on page 38

Christmas Place Mat Set

Continued from page 37

times, ch 4, sc in next joining, ch 4, sc in next ch sp, (ch 2, sc in corresponding ch-4 sp on last Block, ch 2, sc in next ch-4 sp on this Block) 3 times, ch 4, (sc in next ch-4 sp or joining, ch 4) around, join with sl st in first sc, fasten off.

Work Second Block 2 more times for a total of 4 Blocks.

Second Row
First Block

Joining to bottom of First Block on last row, repeat First Row Second Block.

Second Block

Join white with sc in ch-4 sp indicated on Motif Joining Diagram, working on bottom of next Block on row above, *(ch 2, sc in corresponding ch-4 sp on other Block, ch 2, sc in next ch-4 sp on this Block) 3 times, ch 4, sc in next joining, ch 4, sc in next ch sp, (ch 2, sc in corresponding ch-4 sp on other Block, ch 2, sc in next ch-4 sp on this Block) 3 times, ch 4, sc in next ch sp*; working on side of last Block on this row; repeat between **, ch 4 (sc in next ch sp, ch 4) around, join with sl st in first sc, fasten off.

Repeat Second Block 2 more times.

Repeat Second Row one more time for a total of 3 rows.

Edging

Working around outer edge, join white with sc in any ch-4 sp, ch 7, sl st in 5th ch from hook, ch 2, (sc in next ch-4 sp, ch 7, sl st in 5th ch from hook, ch 2) around, join with sl st in first sc, fasten off.

COASTER

Block

Work same as Place Mat Block.

Edging

Rnd 1: Working around entire outer edge of one Block, join white with sc in upper right corner ch-4 sp (see Motif Joining Diagram), ch 4, (sc in next ch sp or joining, ch 4) around, join with sl st in first sc, fasten off.

Rnd 2: Working around outer edge, join white with sc in any ch 4 sp, ch 7, sl st in 5th ch from hook, ch 2, (sc in next ch-4 sp, ch 7, sl st in 5th ch from hook, ch 2) around, join with sl st in first sc, fasten off. •

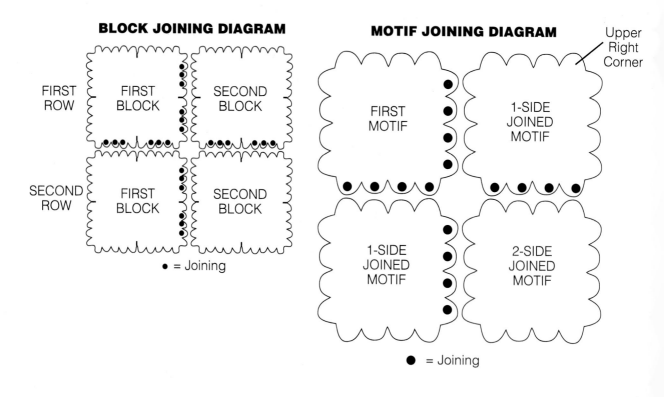

BLOCK JOINING DIAGRAM

FIRST ROW — FIRST BLOCK / SECOND BLOCK

SECOND ROW — FIRST BLOCK / SECOND BLOCK

• = Joining

MOTIF JOINING DIAGRAM

Upper Right Corner

FIRST MOTIF / 1-SIDE JOINED MOTIF

1-SIDE JOINED MOTIF / 2-SIDE JOINED MOTIF

● = Joining

Quick Chick

Designed by Sandra Miller-Maxfield

Finished Size

Chick is 4½" tall.

Materials

- ❍ Fuzzy sport yarn — small amount each yellow and orange
- ❍ One small squeaker
- ❍ 2 red 6-mm. beads
- ❍ Polyester fiberfill
- ❍ Tapestry needle
- ❍ G crochet hook or size needed to obtain gauge

Gauge

4 sc sts = 1"; 4 sc rows = 1".

Body and Head

Note: Do not join rnds unless otherwise stated. Mark first st of each rnd.

Rnd 1: Starting at **bottom of Body,** with yellow, ch 2, 6 sc in 2nd ch from hook (6).

Rnd 2: 2 sc in each st around (12).

Rnd 3: (Sc in next st, 2 sc in next st) around (18).

Rnd 4: Sc in each st around.

Rnd 5: 2 sc in each of first 2 sts, (sc in next 6 sts, 2 sc in each of next 2 sts) around (24).

Rnd 6: Sc in first 11 sts, 2 sc in each of next 2 sts, sc in last 11 sts (26).

Rnd 7: Sc in first 12 sts, 2 sc in each of next 2 sts, sc in last 12 sts (28).

Rnd 8: 2 sc in each of first 2 sts, sc in next 6 sts, 2 sc in next st, sc in next 10 sts, 2 sc in next st, sc in next 6 sts, 2 sc in each of last 2 sts (34).

Rnd 9: Repeat rnd 4.

Rnd 10: 2 sc in first st, sc in next 14 sts, (sc next 2 sts tog) 2 times, sc in next 14 sts, 2 sc in last st (34).

Rnd 11: Repeat rnd 4.

Rnd 12: Sc first 2 sts tog, sc in next 13 sts, (sc next 2 sts tog) 2 times, sc in next 13 sts, sc last 2 sts tog (30).

Rnd 13: Sc first 2 sts tog, sc in each st around to last 2 sts, sc last 2 sts tog (28).

Rnd 14: For **head,** sl st in first 6 sts, sc in next 16 sts, skip next 6 sts, skip first 6 sl sts, join with sl st in first sc (16 sc).

Rnd 15: Ch 1, sc in first 4 sts, 2 sc in next st, sc in next 6 sts, 2 sc in next st, sc in last 4 sts, join (18).

Rnds 16-17: Ch 1, sc in each st around, join.

Rnd 18: Ch 1, sc first 2 sts tog, sc in each st around to last 2 sts, sc last 2 sts tog, join (16).

Rnd 19: Ch 1, (sc next 2 sts tog) 2 times, *sc in each of next 2 sts, (sc next 2 sts tog) 2 times; repeat from *, join (10).

Continued on page 59

Floral Gift Box

Designed by Kathy Wigington

Finished Size

Gift Box is 8½" across.

Materials

- ○ Worsted-weight yarn —
  2 ozs. white
- ○ Size 10 bedspread cotton —
  60 yds. pink and
  15 yds. green
- ○ 9" satin ¼" ribbon
- ○ Fabric stiffener
- ○ Tapestry needle
- ○ No. 7 steel and H crochet
  hooks or size needed to
  obtain gauge

Gauge

With **H hook and worsted-weight yarn,** 3 dc sts = 1"; 2 dc rows = 1"

Box Bottom

Row 1: With white, ch 4, 4 dc in 4th ch from hook, turn (5 dc).

Row 2: Ch 3, dc in same st, (dc in next st, 2 dc in next st) across, turn (8).

Rows 3-11: Ch 3, dc in same st, dc in each st across with 2 dc in last st, turn, ending with 26 sts in last row.

Row 12: For **first half,** ch 2, dc in next 9 sts, dc next 2 sts tog leaving remaining sts unworked, turn (10).

Row 13: Ch 3, dc in each st across, turn.

Row 14: Ch 1, sl st in first st, sc in next st, hdc in next st, dc in next 4 sts, hdc in next st, sc in next st, sl st in last st, fasten off.

Row 12: For **second half,**

skip next 2 sts, join white with sl st in next st, ch 2, dc in each st across to last 2 sts, dc last 2 sts tog, turn (10).

Rows 13-14: Repeat same rows of first half. **Do not fasten off** at end of last row.

Rnd 15: Working around outer edge of heart, ch 1, 2 sc in end of each row and sc in each st around with 3 sc in tip of heart, join with sl st in first sc (86).

Rnd 16: Working this rnd in **back lps** only, ch 3, dc in each st around, join with sl st in top of ch-3.

Rnd 17: Ch 3, dc in each st around, join, fasten off.

Box Top

Rows 1-11: Repeat same rows of Box Bottom.

Row 12: For **first half,** ch 2, dc in next 10 sts, dc next 2 sts tog leaving remaining sts unworked, turn (11).

Row 13: Ch 3, dc in each st across, turn.

Row 14: Ch 1, sl st in first st, sc in next st, hdc in next st, dc in next 5 sts, hdc in next st, sc in next st, sl st in last st, fasten off.

Row 12: For **second half,** join white with sl st in next st, ch 2, dc in each st across to last 2 sts, dc last 2 sts tog, turn (11).

Rows 13-14: Repeat same rows of first half. **Do not fasten off** at end of last row.

Rnd 15: Working around outer edge of heart, ch 2, 2 hdc in end of each row and hdc in each st around with 3 hdc in tip of heart, join with sl st in top of ch-2 (88).

Rnd 16: Working this rnd in **back lps,** ch 2, hdc in each st around, join, fasten off.

Trim

Rnd 1: Working in **front lps** of rnd 15 on Box Top, with No. 7 steel hook, join pink with sc in any st, (ch 6, skip next st, sc in next st) around; to **join,** ch 3, dc in first sc (44 ch sps).

Rnd 2: Ch 1, sc around joining dc, (ch 6, sc in next ch sp) around, join as before.

Note: For **picot,** ch 3, sl st in 3rd ch from hook.

Rnd 3: Ch 1, sc around joining dc, (ch 2, picot, ch 2) in next ch sp, *sc in next ch sp, (ch 2, picot, ch 2) in next ch sp; repeat from * around, join with sl st in first sc, fasten off.

Flower (make 3)

Notes: For **small petal (sm petal),** (sc, hdc, 3 dc, hdc, sc) in next ch.

For **medium petal (med petal),** (sc, hdc, 5 dc, hdc, sc) in next ch.

For **large petal (lg petal),** (sc, hdc, dc, 3 tr, dc, hdc, sc) in next ch.

For **extra large petal (x-lg petal),** sc, hdc, dc, 5 tr, dc, hdc, sc) in next ch.

With pink, ch 24, sm petal in 2nd ch from hook, (skip next ch, sm petal in next ch) 2 times, (skip next ch, med petal in next ch) 3 times, (skip next ch, lg petal in next ch) 3 times, (skip next ch, x-lg petal in next

Continued on page 59

Pastel Gift Baskets

Designed by Kathy Wigington

CHECKERED BASKET

Finished Size

Basket is 9½"– long and 3½"– tall not including Handle.

Materials

- ○ Worsted-weight yarn — 3 oz. white, 1 oz. each green and yellow
- ○ Two 18" pieces 16-gauge wire
- ○ Sewing thread
- ○ Sewing and tapestry needles
- ○ J crochet hook or size needed to obtain gauge

Gauge

With 2 strands yarn held together, 3 dc = 1"; 3 dc rows = 2".
Notes: Use 2 strands same color yarn held together throughout.
When changing colors (see page 158), work over dropped color and carry across to each color section.
Fasten off colors when no longer needed.

Basket
Base

Row 1: With white, ch 29, sc in 2nd ch from hook, sc in each ch across, turn (28 sc).
Rows 2-16: Ch 1, sc in each st across, turn. At end of last row, **do not turn,** fasten off.

Sides

Rnd 1: Working around outer edge of Base, working in **back lps** of row 16, join green with sl st in first st, ch 3, dc in each of next 3 sts changing to white in last st made, dc in each of next 2 sts changing to green in last st made, (dc in next 4 sts changing to white in last st made, dc in each of next 2 sts changing to green in last st made) 3 times, dc in each of next 3 sts, 2 dc in next st, dc in each of next 3 rows changing to white in last st made, dc in each of next 2 rows changing to green in last st made, dc in next 4 rows changing to white in last st made, dc in each of next 2 rows changing to green in last st made, dc in each of next 3 rows, 2 dc in next st, dc in each of next 3 sts changing to white in last st made, continue working in established color pattern around, join with sl st in top of ch-3, fasten off both colors (88 dc).
Rnd 2: Join yellow with sl st in first st, ch 3 change to white, *dc in each of next 2 sts changing to yellow in last st made, (dc in next 4 sts changing to white in last st made, dc in each of next 2 sts changing to yellow in last st made) 4 times, dc in each of next 2 sts changing to white in last st made, dc in each of next 2 sts changing to yellow in last st made; repeat between ( ) 2 more times*, dc in each of next 2 sts changing to white in last st made; repeat between ** one more time, dc in last st, join, fasten off both colors.

Rnd 3: Working in color pattern established in rnd 1, ch 3, dc in each st around changing colors as colors change in rnd 1, join, fasten off both colors.
Rnds 4-5: Repeat rnds 2 and 3.
Rnd 6: Join white with sc in first st; working left to right, **reverse sc** (see page 159), in each st around, join with sl st in first sc, fasten off.

Handle

Row 1: With green, ch 62, dc in 4th ch from hook, dc in each ch across, fasten off (60 dc).
Row 2: Working over one piece of wire (see illustration), join white with sc in **last** st of row 1, reverse sc in each st across, fasten off.
Row 3: Working in starting ch on opposite side of row 1, repeat row 2.
Fold ½" on ends of wire to inside of Handle. Tack Handle to rnds 1-5 centered inside long edges of Basket.

SC OVER WIRE

Continued on page 44

Pastel Gift Baskets

Continued from page 42

RUFFLED BASKET

Finished Size

Basket is 4" tall not including handle.

Materials

○ Worsted-weight yarn — 2½" oz. each white and green, 1 oz. each yellow and peach
○ Three 18" pieces 16-gauge wire
○ Craft glue or hot glue gun
○ Tapestry needle
○ G and J crochet hooks or size needed to obtain gauge

Gauge

With **J hook and 2 strands yarn held together,** rnd 1 = ¾" across; 3 sc rows = 1".
Notes: Use J hook and 2 strands same color yarn held together unless otherwise stated.
Do not join rnds unless otherwise stated. Mark first st of each rnd.

Basket

Rnd 1: With white, ch 2, 8 sc in 2nd ch from hook (8 sc).
Rnd 2: 2 sc in each st around (16).
Rnd 3: (Sc in next st, 2 sc in next st) around (24).
Rnd 4: (Sc in each of next 2 sts, 2 sc in next st) around (32).
Rnd 5: (Sc in each of next 3 sts, 2 sc in next st) around, join with sl st in first sc (40).
Rnd 6: Working this rnd in **back lps** only, ch 1, sc in first st, hdc in next st, 3 dc in next st, hdc in next st, (sc in each of next 2 sts, hdc in next st, 3 dc in next st, hdc in next st) around to last st, sc in last st, join, fasten off (56 sts).
Rnd 7: Join green with sl st in last hdc made, ch 3, tr next 2 sts tog, dc in next st, hdc in next st, 3 sc in next st, hdc in next st, (dc in next st, tr next 2 sts tog, dc in next st, hdc in next st, 3 sc in next st, hdc in next st) around, join with sl st in top of ch-3, fasten off (64).
Rnd 8: Join white with sc in first st, sc in next 2 sts, hdc in next st, dc in next st, 3 dc in next st, dc in next st, hdc in next st, (sc in next 3 sts, hdc in next st, dc in next st, 3 dc in next st, dc in next st, hdc in next st) around, join with sl st in first sc, fasten off (80).
Rnd 9: Join yellow with sl st in last hdc made, ch 3, tr next 3 sts tog, dc in next st, hdc in next st, sc in next st, 3 sc in next st, sc in next st, hdc in next st, (dc in next st, tr next 3 sts tog, dc in next st, hdc in next st, sc in next st, 3 sc in next st, sc in next st, hdc in next st) around, join with sl st in top of ch-3, fasten off.
Rnd 10: Join white with sl st in first st, ch 1, sc first 3 sts tog, hdc in next st, dc in each of next 2 sts, 3 dc in next st, dc in each of next 2 sts, hdc in next st, (sc next 3 sts tog, hdc in next st, dc in each of next 2 sts, 3 dc in next st, dc in each of next 2 sts, hdc in next st) around, join with sl st in first sc, fasten off.
Rnd 11: Join peach with sl st in last dc made, ch 3, tr next 3 sts tog, dc in next st, hdc in next st, sc in next st, 3 sc in next st, sc in next st, hdc in next st, (dc in next st, tr next 3 sts tog, dc in next st, hdc in next st, sc in next st, 3 sc in next st, sc in next st, hdc in next st) around, join with sl st in top of ch-3, fasten off.
Rnd 12: Join white with sc in last hdc made, sc next 3 sts tog, sc in next st, hdc in next st, dc in next st, 3 dc in next st, dc in next st, hdc in next st, (sc in next st, sc next 3 sts tog, sc in next st, hdc in next st, dc in next st, 3 dc in next st, dc in next st, hdc in next st) around, join with sl st in first sc, fasten off.
Rnd 13: With green, repeat rnd 9.
Rnd 14: Join white with sl st in last hdc made, ch 4, skip next st, (sl st in next st, ch 4, skip next st) around, join with sl st in first sl st (40 ch sps).
Rnd 15: Sl st in first ch sp, ch 1, (sc, hdc, dc, hdc, sc) in each ch sp around, join with sl st in first sc, fasten off.

Handle

For **each piece,** with G hook and 2 strands yellow held together, join with sc around one piece of wire (see illustration on page 44), sc around wire covering completely, fasten off.

Glue sc on each end of wire to secure. Repeat with green and peach on remaining wires. Braid all 3 pieces together, tack ends to rnd 9 on inside of Basket.

TULIP BASKET

Finished Size

Basket is 8" across bottom and 4" tall not including handle.

Materials

○ Worsted-weight yarn — 3 oz. white, 1 oz. each green and yellow, small amount pink
○ 1" x 20" piece of plastic canvas
○ 22" pink ¼" satin ribbon
○ Pink sewing thread
○ Sewing and tapestry needles
○ G and J crochet hooks or sizes needed to obtain gauges

Gauges

With **G hook and 2 strands**

held tog, 4 sc = 1"; 4 sc rows = 1". With **J hook and 2 strands held together,** 3 sc = 1"; 3 sc rows = 1".

Basket

Notes: Use 2 strands same color yarn held together unless otherwise stated.

Use J hook unless otherwise stated.

Rnd 1: Starting at **bottom,** with white, ch 2, 6 sc in 2nd ch from hook (6 sc).

Rnd 2: 2 sc in each st around (12).

Rnd 3: (Sc in next st, 2 sc in next st) around (18).

Rnd 4: (Sc in each of next 2 sts, 2 sc in next st) around (24).

Rnd 5: (Sc in next 3 sts, 2 sc in next st) around (30).

Rnd 6: (Sc in next 4 sts, 2 sc in next st) around (36).

Rnd 7: (Sc in next 5 sts, 2 sc in next st) around (42).

Rnd 8: (Sc in next 6 sts, 2 sc in next st) around (48).

Rnd 9: (Sc in next 7 sts, 2 sc in next st) around (54).

Rnd 10: (Sc in next 8 sts, 2 sc in next st) around (60).

Rnd 11: (Sc in next 9 sts, 2 sc in next st) around (66).

Rnd 12: (Sc in next 10 sts, 2 sc in next st) around, join with sl st in first sc, fasten off (72).

Rnd 13: Working this rnd in **back lps** only, join green with sc in first st, sc in each st around, join with sl st in first sc, fasten off.

Rnd 14: Join yellow with sc in first st, sc in each st around, join.

Rnd 15: Ch 1, sc in each st around, join, fasten off.

Rnd 16: Join white with sc in first st, sc in each st around, join.

Rnds 17-21: Ch 1, sc in each st around, join. At end of last rnd, fasten off.

Rnds 22-23: Repeat rnds 14-15.

Rnd 24: Join green with sc in first st; working left to right, **reverse sc** (see page 159) in each st around, join, fasten off.

For **trim,** with bottom facing you, working in **front lps** of rnd 12, join green with sl st in any st, sl st in each st around, join with sl st in first sl st, fasten off.

Tulip (make 9)

Note: Use G hook and one strand of yarn for reminder of pattern.

Row 1: With pink, ch 3, sc in 2nd ch from hook, sc in last ch, turn (2 sc).

Row 2: Ch 1, 2 sc in first st, sc in last st, turn.

Row 3: Ch 3, sl st in 2nd ch from hook, sl st in last ch, *sl st in next st on row 2, ch 3, sl st in 2nd ch from hook, sl st in last ch; repeat from *, sl st in same st on row 2, fasten off.

Leaf (make 9)

With green, ch 12, sl st in 2nd ch from hook, sc in next 4 chs, 3 sc in next ch, sc in next 4 chs, sl st in last ch, fasten off.

Sew Tulips and Leaves evenly spaced around rnds 17-20 as shown in photo.

Handle Side (make 2)

Row 1: With green, ch 82, sc in 2nd ch from hook, sc in each ch across, turn, fasten off (80).

Row 2: Join yellow with sc in first st, sc in each st across, turn, fasten off.

Row 3: Join white with sl st in first st, ch 3, skip next st, hdc in next st, (ch 1, skip next st, hdc in next st) across, turn, fasten off (41 hdc, 40 ch sps).

Row 4: Join yellow with sc in first ch sp, sc in each hdc in each ch sp across, turn, fasten off (80).

Row 5: Join green with sc in first st, sc in each st across, turn.

Row 6: Working this row in **back lps,** ch 1, sc in each st across, turn, fasten off.

Row 7: Repeat row 2.

Row 8: Join white with sl st in first st, ch 2, hdc in each st across, turn, fasten off.

Row 9: Repeat row 2.

Row 10: Repeat row 5, fasten off.

Weave ribbon through hdc of row 3 on one Side. Turn ends under; tack in place. Holding Sides wrong sides together with plastic canvas strip between, matching sts, sew long edges together. Tack Handle ends to rnds 13-23 on inside of Basket. •

Keepsake Tablecloth

Designed by Gloria Coombes

Finished Size

Tablecloth is 55" square.

Materials

○ Size 10 bedspread cotton —
3,700 yds. white
○ Tapestry needle
○ No. 9 steel crochet hook or
size needed to obtain gauge

Gauge

Rnd 1 of Large Motif No. 1 = ¾"
across. Each Large Motif is
5" across when blocked.

Note: Tablecloth may ruffle until
blocked.

Large Motif No. 1

Rnd 1: Ch 6, sl st in first ch to
form ring, ch 3, 15 dc in ring,
join with sl st in top of ch-3
(16 dc).

Rnd 2: (Ch 3, dc) in first st, ch
3, skip next st, (2 dc in next
st, ch 3, skip next st) around,
join (16 dc, 8 ch-3 sps).

Notes: For **picot,** ch 5, sl st in
5th ch from hook.

For **triple treble (tr tr),** yo 4
times, insert hook in st, yo,
draw lp through, (yo, draw
through 2 lps on hook) 5 times.

Rnd 3: Ch 1, sc in first st, ch 8,
sl st in 5th ch from hook, picot
2 times, ch 3, sc in next dc,
(ch 11, skip next ch-3 sp, sc

in next dc, ch 8, sl st in 5th ch
from hook, picot 2 times, ch
3, sc in next dc) around to last
ch-3 sp; to **join,** ch 6, skip
same ch-3 sp, tr tr in first sc
(24 picots, 8 ch-11 lps).

Rnd 4: Ch 8, skip next picot,
sc in next picot, ch 5, skip
next picot, (dc in 6th ch of
next ch-11 lp, ch 5, skip next
picot, sc in next picot, ch 5,
skip next picot) around, join
with sl st in 3rd ch of ch-8
(16 ch-5 sps, 8 dc, 8 sc).

Rnd 5: (Ch 3, dc) in first st, ch 6,
skip next ch-5 sp, sc in next sc,
picot, ch 6, skip next ch-5 sp,
(2 dc in next dc, ch 6, skip next
ch-5 sp, sc in next sc, picot, ch
6, skip next ch-5 sp) around,
join with sl st in top of ch-3 (16
dc, 16 ch-6 sps, 8 picot).

Rnd 6: Ch 1, sc in first st, ch 8,
sl st in 5th ch from hook, picot
2 times, ch 3, sc in next dc,
ch 7, skip next ch-6 sp, sc in
next picot, picot (ch 7, skip
next ch-6 sp, sc in next dc, ch
8, sl st in 5th ch from hook,
picot 2 times, ch 3, sc in next
dc, ch 7, skip next ch-6 sp, sc
in next picot, picot) around; to
join, ch 3, tr in first sc (32
picots, 16 ch-7 sps).

Rnd 7: Ch 1, sc around joining
tr, ch 9, skip next picot, sc in
next picot, picot, ch 9, skip
next picot, sc in 4th ch of next
ch-7 sp, ch 5, dc in next

picot, picot, ch 5, (sc in 4th
ch of next ch-7 sp, ch 9, skip
next picot, sc in next picot,
picot, ch 9, skip next picot, sc
in 4th ch of next ch-7 sp, ch
5, dc in next picot, picot, ch
5) around, join with sl st in
first sc, fasten off.

Large Motif Nos. 2-121

Notes: For **joining picot,** ch 2,
sl st in corresponding picot on
next Motif, ch 2, sl st in first ch.

Join Motifs in 11 rows of 11
Motifs each according to
Joining Diagram on page 59.

Rnd 1-6: Repeat same rnds of
Large Motif No. 1.

Rnd 7: Repeat same rnd of
Large Motif No. 1 using
joining picots to join Motifs
together.

Small Motif (make 100)

Note: Join Small Motifs to
spaces between Large Motifs
according to diagram.

Rnds 1-2: Repeat same rnds of
Large Motif No. 1.

Rnd 3: Ch 1, sc in first st, ch 8,
sl st in 5th ch from hook, joining picot, picot, ch 3, sc in
next dc, ch 7, skip next ch-3
sp, (sc in next dc, ch 8, sl st in
5th ch from hook, joining
picot, picot, ch 3, sc in next
dc, ch 7, skip next ch-3 sp)
around, join with sl st in first
sc, fasten off. •

Little Dazzlers

Designed by Katherine Eng

Finished Size

Star is 4¼" across; Wreath is 3¼" across, not including hangers.

Materials For One

○ Size 10 bedspread cotton — 50 yds. center color, 15 yds. trim color A and 12 yds. trim color B or optional 2-ply metallic thread
○ 13" matching ¼" satin ribbon for Wreath
○ Polyester fiberfill
○ No. 11 steel crochet hook or size needed to obtain gauge

Gauge

9 sc = 1".

Star
Side (make 2)

Rnd 1: With center color, ch 4, sl st in first ch to form ring, ch 1, 8 sc in ring, join with sl st in first sc (8 sc).

Rnd 2: Ch 1, 2 sc in each st around, join (16).

Rnd 3: Ch 1, sc in first st, 2 sc next st, (sc in next st, 2 sc in next st) around, join (24).

Rnd 4: Ch 1, sc in first st, skip next st, 5 dc in next st, skip next st, (sc in next st, skip next st, 5 dc in next st, skip next st) around, join (30 dc, 6 sc).

Rnd 5: Ch 3, 6 dc in same st, sc in center st of next 5-dc group, (7 dc in next sc, sc in center st of next 5-dc group) around, join with sl st in top of ch-3.

Rnd 6: Ch 1, sc in each st around with (sc, ch 2, sc) in center st of each 7-dc group,

join with sl st in first sc (54 sc, 6 ch-2 sps).

Rnd 7: Ch 1, sc in first st, *[hdc in each of next 2 sts, dc in next st, (2 tr, ch 2, 2 tr) in next ch-2 sp, dc in next st, hdc in each of next 2 sts], sc in each of next 3 sts; repeat from * 4 more times; repeat between [ ], sc in each of last 2 sts, join.

Rnd 8: Ch 1, sc in each st around with (2 sc, ch 2, 2 sc) in each ch-2 sp, join, fasten off (102 sc, 6 ch-2 sps).

Rnd 9: Join trim color A with sc in any ch-2 sp, (2 sc, ch 2, 2 sc) in same sp, *[sc in next 8 sts, skip next st, sc in next 8 sts], (2 sc, ch 2, 2 sc) in next ch-2 sp; repeat from * 4 more times; repeat between [ ], join, fasten off.

Rnd 10: Hold Sides wrong sides together, matching sts; working through both thicknesses, join trim color B with sc in any ch-2 sp; for **hanger loop,** ch 60, sl st in 3rd ch of ch-60, ch 2, sc in same ch sp as last sc; *[(ch 3, skip next st, sc in next st) 5 times, (sc in next st, ch 3, skip next st) 5 times], (sc, ch 3, sc) in next ch-2 sp; repeat from * 4 more times; repeat between [ ] stuffing before closing, join, fasten off.

Wreath

Rnd 1: For **first side,** with center color, ch 30, sl st in first ch to form ring, ch 1, sc in each ch around, join with sl st in first sc (30 sc).

Rnd 2: Ch 1, 2 sc in each st around, join (60).

Rnd 3: Ch 1, sc in first st, skip

next 2 sts, 5 dc in next st, skip next 2 sts, (sc in next st, skip next 2 sts, 5 dc in next st, skip next 2 sts) around, join.

Rnd 4: Ch 3, 6 dc in same st, sc in center st of next 5-dc group, (7 dc in next sc, sc in center st of next 5-dc group) around, join with sl st in top of ch-3.

Rnd 5: Ch 3, (*hdc in next st, sc in each of next 3 sts, hdc in next st*, dc in each of next 3 sts) around to last 7 sts; repeat between **, dc in each of last 2 sts, join.

Rnd 6: Ch 1, sc in each st around, join with sl st in first sc, fasten off (80).

Rnd 7: Join trim color A with sc in any st, sc in each st around, join, fasten off.

Rnd 8: For **second side,** with wrong side of first side facing you, working in starting ch on opposite side of rnd 1, join center color with sc in first ch, sc in each ch around, join (30 sc).

Rnd 9-14: Repeat rnds 2-7.

Rnd 15: Hold rnds 7 and 14 wrong sides together, matching sts, working through both thicknesses, join trim color B with sc in any st, ch 2, sc in same st, skip next st, *(sc, ch 2, sc) in next st, skip next st; repeat from * around to last 2 sts stuffing as you work, sc in next st; for **hanging loop,** ch 60, sl st in 3rd ch of ch-60, ch 2, sc in same st as last sc, skip last st, join, fasten off.

Tie ribbon into a bow around st at bottom of center opening as shown in photo. •

Gifts for the Holidays

Bride's Cross

Designed by Shep Shephard

Finished Size

Cross is 5" x 7".

Materials

- ○ Size 10 bedspread cotton — 30 yds. white
- ○ 28 gold 4-mm beads
- ○ 14 white 3-mm beads
- ○ 1 yd. white 4-mm strung beads
- ○ 1 yd. white ⅛" ribbon
- ○ 2 plastic wedding bands
- ○ White sewing thread
- ○ Sewing needle
- ○ No. 9 steel crochet hook or size needed to obtain gauge

Gauge

Each Motif is 1¼" square.

First Motif

Rnd 1: Ch 7, sl st in first ch to form ring, ch 1, (sc, ch 3, 2 dc, ch 1, 2 dc, ch 3) 4 times in ring, join with sl st in first sc (16 dc, 4 sc, 4-ch-1 sps).

Rnd 2: Ch 6, (sc, ch 3, sc) in next ch-1 sp, ch 3, *dc in next sc, ch 3, (sc, ch 3, sc) in next ch-1 sp, ch 3; repeat from * around, join with sl st in 3rd ch of ch-6.

Rnd 3: Ch 1, sc in first st, ch 3, skip next ch-3 sp; for **corner,** (3 dc, ch 3, 3 dc) in next ch-3 sp, ch 3, skip next ch-3 sp, *sc in next dc, ch 3, skip next ch-3 sp; for **corner,** (3 dc, ch 3, 3 dc) in next ch-3 sp; ch 3, skip next ch-3 sp; repeat from * around, join with sl st in first sc, fasten off.

Second Motif

Rnds 1-2: Repeat same rnds of First Motif.

Rnd 3: Ch 1, sc in first st, ch 3, skip next ch-3 sp, (3 dc, ch 1) in next ch-3 sp, sl st in any corner ch-3 sp on last Motif, ch 1, 3 dc in same ch sp on this Motif, ch 1, sl st in next ch-3 sp on last Motif, ch 1, sc in next dc on this Motif, ch 1, sl st in next ch-3 sp on last Motif, ch 1, skip next ch-3 sp on this Motif, 3 dc in next ch-3 sp, ch 1, sl st in next corner ch-3 sp on last Motif, ch 1, 3 dc in same ch sp on this Motif, ch 3, skip next ch-3 sp, *sc in next dc, ch 3, skip next ch-3 sp, (3 dc, ch 3, 3 dc) in next ch-1 sp, ch 3, skip next ch-3 sp; repeat from *, join with sl st in first sc, fasten off.

Repeat Second Motif on each remaining side of First Motif. Repeat Second Motif on opposite side of joining on one Second Motif.

Border

Note: For **picot,** (sl st, ch 3, sl st, ch 4, sl st, ch 3, sl st) in next ch sp or next joining.

Join with sl st in any corner ch sp, (ch 3, sl st, ch 4, sl st, ch 3, sl st) in same sp, skipping sc sts throughout, sc in each dc and 3 sc in each ch sp around with picot in each outside corner ch sp, in each inside corner and in each joining between Motifs on leg of Cross, join with sl st in first sc, fasten off.

Sew one white bead and 2 gold beads to each picot as shown in photo.

With strung beads and ribbon held together, tie into a bow, tack to center of Cross.

Tie wedding bands to ends of ribbons. ●

Heart Ornaments

Designed by Margaret Coffey

Finished Size

Each Heart is 3¼" x 3½".

Materials

○ Size 10 bedspread cotton —
  25 yds. desired color
○ 12" invisible thread or
  fishing line
○ Liquid fabric stiffener
○ Styrofoam® or blocking board
○ Plastic wrap
○ Rustproof pins
○ No. 8 steel crochet hook or
  size needed to obtain gauge

Gauge

Rnd 1 of Heart A is 1⅜" across.
  Rnds 1-3 of Heart B are 1"
  across. Rnds 1-2 of Heart C
  are ⅞" across.

Heart A
Note: For **cluster (cl),** * yo 2
  times, insert hook in ring, yo,
  draw lp through, (yo, draw
  through 2 lps on hook) 2
  times; repeat from *, yo, draw
  through all 3 lps on hook.
Rnd 1: Ch 6, sl st in first ch to
  form ring, ch 4, tr in ring, (ch 5,
  cl in ring) 7 times; to **join,** ch 2,
  dc in top of first tr (8 ch sps).
Rnd 2: Ch 1, sc around joining
  dc, (ch 7, sc in next ch sp)
  around; to **join,** ch 3, tr in
  first sc.
Notes: For **double treble crochet (dtr),** yo 3 times insert
  hook in next ch sp, yo, draw
  lp through, (yo, draw through
  2 lps on hook) 4 times.
For **triple treble crochet (ttr),**

yo 4 times, insert hook in next
  ch sp, yo, draw lp through,
  (yo, draw through 2 lps on
  hook) 5 times.
Rnd 3: Ch 1, sc around joining
  tr, *ch 5, (dtr, ch 5, ttr, ch 5,
  ttr, ch 5, dtr) in next ch sp, ch
  5*, tr in next ch sp, ch 5, dc
  in next ch sp, ch 5, (tr, ch 5,
  dtr, ch 5, tr) in next ch sp, ch
  5, dc in next ch sp, ch 5, tr in
  next ch sp; repeat between
  **, join with sl st in first sc
  (16 sts, 16 ch-5 sps).
Note: For **love knot (lk,** see
  illustration) draw up long lp
  on hook, yo, draw lp through,
  sc in back strand of long lp.
Rnd 4: Ch 1, sc in first st, lk,
  *[sc in next st, lk, (sc in next
  ch sp, lk) 2 times, sc in next
  st, lk], (sc in next ch sp, lk) 4
  times; repeat from *; repeat
  between [ ], join, fasten off.

Heart B
Rnd 1: Ch 6, sl st in first ch to
  form ring, ch 1, 8 sc in ring,
  join with sl st in first sc (8 sc).
Rnd 2: Ch 1, sc in first st, ch 2,
  (sc in next st, ch 2) around, join.
Rnd 3: For **petals,** sl st in first
  ch sp, ch 1, (sc, 3 dc, sc) in
  same sp and in each ch sp
  around, join (6 petals).
Rnd 4: Working behind petals in
  skipped sts of rnd 2, sl st in
  first st, ch 1, sc in same sp,
  (ch 5, sc in next st) around; to
  join, ch 2, dc in first sc.
Rnds 5-7: Repeat rnds 2-4 of
  Heart A.

Heart C
Rnd 1: Repeat rnd 1 of Heart B.

Rnd 2: Ch 1, sc in first st, (ch 5,
  sc in next st) around; to **join,**
  ch 2, dc in first sc (8 ch sps).
Rnd 3: Ch 1, sc around joining
  dc, lk, (sc in next ch sp, lk)
  around, join with sl st in first sc.
Rnd 4: Ch 1, sc in first sc, (ch
  7, sc in next sc) around; to
  join, ch 3, tr in first sc.
Rnds 5-6: Repeat rnds 3 and 4 of
  Heart A.

Finishing
1: Apply liquid fabric stiffener to
  each Heart according to manufacturer's instructions. Pin to
  plastic-covered blocking board,
  shape. Let dry completely.
2: For each **hanging loop,** tie
  knot in ends of fishing line,
  fold in half, insert fold from
  back to front around top sc on
  rnd before last pulling fold to
  back, insert tied ends through
  fold, pull tight. •

LOVE KNOT ILLUSTRATION

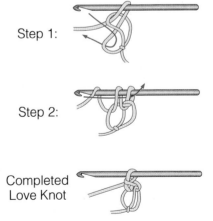

Step 1:

Step 2:

Completed
Love Knot

Rose Sachet

Designed by Jo Ann Maxwell

Finished Size

Sachet is 5½" across.

Materials

- ◯ Size 10 bedspread cotton — 100 yds cream and 50 yds. pink
- ◯ 18" pink ⅜" satin ribbon
- ◯ 8" piece gold cord
- ◯ 9 white 6-mm pearl beads
- ◯ 10" circle of pink tulle
- ◯ Potpourri
- ◯ Styrofoam® or blocking board
- ◯ Plastic wrap
- ◯ Spray starch
- ◯ Rustproof pins
- ◯ Pink sewing thread
- ◯ Sewing and tapestry needles
- ◯ No. 5 steel crochet hook or size needed to obtain gauge

Gauge

Rnds 1-4 = 2" across.

Side (make 2)

Rnd 1: With pink, ch 4, sl st in first ch to form ring, ch 4, (hdc in ring, ch 2) 7 times, join with sl st in 2nd ch of ch-4 (8 hdc, 8 ch-2 sps).

Rnd 2: Sl st in first ch-2 sp, ch 1, (sc, hdc, 4 dc, hdc, sc) in same sp and in each ch-2 sp around, **do not join** (8 petals).

Rnd 3: Working behind last rnd, (sc around post of next sc between petals on rnd before last, ch 3) around, join with sl st in first sc (8 ch-2 sps).

Rnd 4: Sl st in first ch-3 sp, ch 1, (sc, hdc, 6 dc, hdc, sc) in same sp and in each ch-3 sp around, join, fasten off (8 petals).

Notes: For **beginning V-stitch (beg V-st),** ch 5, dc in same st.

For **V-stitch (V-st)** (dc, ch 2, dc) in next st.

Rnd 5: Join cream with sl st in first sc of any petal, beg V-st, ch 5, (V-st in first sc of next petal, ch 5) around, join with sl st in 3rd ch of beg V-st (8 V-sts, 8 ch-5 sps).

Notes: For **beginning shell (beg shell),** ch 3, (dc, ch 2, 2 dc) in same sp.

For **shell,** (2 dc, ch 2, 2 dc) in next ch sp.

For **picot,** ch 3, sl st in top of last st made.

Rnd 6: Sl st in ch sp of first V-st, beg shell, ch 2, sc in 3rd ch of next ch-5, picot, ch 2, (shell in ch sp of next V-st, ch 2, sc in 3rd ch of next ch-5, picot, ch 2) around, join with sl st in top of ch-3 (16 ch-2 sps, 8 shells, 8 picot).

Note: For **love knot (lk,** see illustration on page 53) draw up long lp on hook, yo, draw lp through, sc in back strand of long lp.

Rnd 7: Sl st in next st, sl st in next ch sp, beg V-st, *(ch 1, lk, sc in next ch-2 sp, ch 5, skip next picot, sc in next ch-2 sp, ch 1 lk*, V-st in ch sp of next shell) 7 times; repeat between **, join with sl st in 3rd ch of beg V-st.

Rnd 8: Sl st in ch sp of beg V-st, ch 5, dc in same sp, (ch 2, dc in same sp) 3 times, ch 2, skip next lk, sc in next ch-5 sp, picot, ch 2, skip next lk, *dc in next V-st, (ch 2, dc in same sp) 4 times, ch 2, skip next lk, sc in next ch-5 sp, picot, ch 2, skip next lk; repeat from * around, join with sl st in 3rd ch of ch-5.

Rnd 9: Ch 1, sc in first st, ch 3, sc in next dc, ch 3, *[(dc, ch 3, dc) in next dc, (ch 3, sc in next dc) 2 times, ch 5, skip next 2 ch-2 sps], (sc in next dc, ch 3) 2 times; repeat from * 6 more times; repeat between [ ], join with sl st in first sc, fasten off.

Finishing

1: Spray both Sides with starch. Pin each to plastic wrapped foam or blocking board, stretching points. Let dry.

2: Baste around outer edge of tulle circle. Pull threads to gather until fabric forms a cup. Fill with about 1 cup of potpourri. Pull threads to close opening, secure. Flatten potpourri bag.

3: To **join,** holding both pieces wrong sides together, weave ribbon through spaces above love knots, inserting potpourri bag before closing. Glue ribbon ends together, trim if necessary.

4: Glue one pearl bead to center of rnd 1 on one Side and one to top of center dc on each point of rnd 8.

5: For **hanger,** glue ends of gold cord inside rnd 8 between Sides. •

Wreath Jar Topper

Designed by Elizabeth Owens

Finished Size

Wreath fits 3" jar opening.

Materials

- ○ Size 10 bedspread cotton — 30 yds. white and 12 yds. green
- ○ 1 gold 3 x 6-mm rice bead
- ○ 1 red rocaille bead
- ○ 5 white 3-mm pearl beads
- ○ 5 red 3-mm pearl beads
- ○ 9" red ⅛" ribbon
- ○ ⅔ yd. red ¼" ribbon
- ○ No. 5 steel crochet hook or size needed to obtain gauge

Gauge

8 sts = 1"; 1 dc or 2 sc rows = ¼".

Topper

Rnd 1: With white, ch 2, 8 sc in 2nd ch from hook, join with sl st in first sc (8 sc).

Rnd 2: Ch 1, 2 sc in each st around, join, fasten off (16).

Rnd 3: Working this rnd in **front lps** only, join green with sc in any st, sc in each st around, join.

Rnd 4: Ch 4, (dc in next st, ch 1) around, join with sl st in 3rd ch of ch-4.

Rnd 5: Ch 1, sc in first st, ch 3, sc in next ch sp, ch 3, (sc in next st, ch 3, sc in next ch sp, ch 3) around, join with sl st in first sc, fasten off (32 ch sps).

Rnd 6: Working on rnd 4, join green with sc around post of any dc, (ch 3, sc around post of same st) 2 times, ch 3, *sc around post of next dc, (ch 3, sc around post of same st) 2 times, ch 3; repeat from * around, join, fasten off.

Rnd 7: Working in ch sps of rnd 5, join white with sc in any ch sp, 2 sc in next ch sp, (sc in next ch sp, 2 sc in next ch sp) around, join (48 sts).

Rnd 8: Ch 3, 2 dc in next st, (dc in next st, 2 dc in next st) around, join with sl st in top of ch-3 (72 dc).

Rnd 9: Ch 1, sc in each st around, join with sl st in first sc.

Rnd 10: Working this rnd in **back lps** only, ch 1, sc in each st around, join.

Rnd 11: Ch 3, dc in each st around, join with sl st in top of ch-3.

Rnds 12-13: Ch 1, sc in each st around, join with sl st in first sc.

Rnd 14: Ch 4, skip next st, (dc in next st, ch 1, skip next st) around, join with sl st in 3rd ch of ch-4.

Rnd 15: Ch 1, sc in first st, ch 3, skip next ch sp, (sc in next st, ch 3, skip next ch sp) around, join with sl st in first sc.

Rnd 16: Sl st in next ch sp, ch 3, 2 dc in same sp, 3 dc in each ch sp around, join with sl st in top of ch-3, fasten off.

Rnd 17: Join green with sc in first st, ch 3, (sc in next st, ch 3) around, join with sl st in first sc, fasten off.

Finishing

1: For candle, sew rocaille bead to center of rnd 1; sew rice bead next to rocaille bead on rnd 2 as shown in photo.

2: Alternating colors, sew pearl beads evenly spaced around rnd 6.

3: Tie ⅛" ribbon into a bow, tack below rice bead.

4: Weave ¼" ribbon through ch sps of rnd 14; tie ends into a bow. •

Snowball Slippers

Designed by Shep Shepherd

Finished Size

Instructions given fit up to Girl's 9" soles. Changes for Girl's 10" soles are in [ ].

Materials

○ Worsted-weight yarn — 3½ [4] ozs. white
○ Tapestry needle
○ I crochet hook or size needed to obtain gauge

Gauge

3 sc = 1"; 3 sc rows = 1".

Slipper (make 2)
Side

Rnd 1: Ch 29 [33], 3 sc in 2nd ch from hook, sc in each ch across with 3 sc in last ch; working on opposite side of ch, sc in each ch across, join with sl st in first sc (58 sc) [66 sc].

Rnd 2: Ch 1, sc in first st, tr in next st, (sc in next st, tr in next st) around, join.

Rnd 3: Ch 4, sc in next st, (tr in next st, sc in next st) around, join with sl st in top of ch-4. First ch-4 counts as first tr.

Rnd 4: Ch 1, sc in first st, tr in next st, (sc in next st, tr in next st) around, join with sl st in first sc.

Rnds 5-8 [5-10]: Repeat rnds 3 and 4 alternately. At end of last rnd, fasten off.

Instep

Rnd 1: Ch 11 [13], 3 sc in 2nd ch from hook, sc in each ch across with 3 sc in last ch; working on opposite side of ch, sc in each ch across, join with sl st in first sc (22 sc)[26 sc].

Rnd 2: Ch 1, (sc, tr) in each st around, join, fasten off.

Leaving 8 [10] sts unworked, matching sts, sew rnd 2 of Instep to rnd 8 [10] on one end of Side.

For **edging,** working around last rnd of Side and across unworked sts of rnd 2 on Instep, join with sc in center back st on Side, sc in each st around with 2 sc in each st across Instep, join with sl st in first sc, fasten off.

Cut 2 strands yarn each 10" long. Holding both strands together, tie into a bow around stitch at center of Instep. •

Quick Chick
Continued from page 39

Rnd 20: Ch 1, skip first st, sc next 2 sts tog, (sc in next st, sc next 2 sts tog) 2 times leaving last st unworked, **do not join** (5).

Rnd 21: Sl st in each st around. Leaving 4" for sewing, fasten off. Sew opening closed.

Place squeaker inside Body of toy being careful not to place fiberfill in front of squeaker opening. (NOTE: If not enough fiberfill is used the squeaker will not inflate; if too much is used it will be difficult for the squeaker to squeak). Test squeaker before you sew opening closed.

Wing (make 2)
Row 1: Ch 5, hdc in 3rd ch from hook, hdc in each of next 2 chs, turn (4).

Row 2: Ch 2, hdc in same st, hdc in each st across with 2 hdc in last st, turn (6).

Row 3: Ch 2, hdc in each st across, turn.

Row 4: Ch 1, sc in first st, hdc in each of next 3 sts, sc in next st, sl st in last st, **do not turn.** Leaving 4" for sewing, fasten off. Sew Wing over rnds 6-12 on each side of Body.

Finishing
1: For **comb,** with orange, ch 6, sc in 2nd ch from hook, sc in next ch, sl st in next ch, 2 sc in next ch, sl st in last ch. Leaving 4" for sewing, fasten off. Sew to top of Head.

2: For **beak,** with orange, ch 3, sc in 2nd ch from hook, sc in last ch. Leaving 4" for sewing, fasten off. Sew to front of Head over rnds 15 and 16.

3: For eyes, sew one bead over rnd 17 on each side of Head. ●

Floral Gift Box
Continued from page 40

ch) 3 times, fasten off (12 petals). Roll into rose shape, tack to secure.

Leaf (make 6)
With No. 7 steel hook and green, ch 9, sc in 2nd ch from hook, hdc in next ch, dc in next 5 chs, 5 hdc in last ch; working on opposite side of ch, dc in next 5 chs, hdc in next ch, sc in last ch, join with sl st in first sc, fasten off.

Finishing
Stiffen all pieces according to manufacturer's instructions, shaping as needed. Let dry. Arrange Flowers, Leaves and ribbon over top of box, glue in place. Let dry. ●

Keepsake Tablecloth
Instructions on page 47

ASSEMBLY DIAGRAM

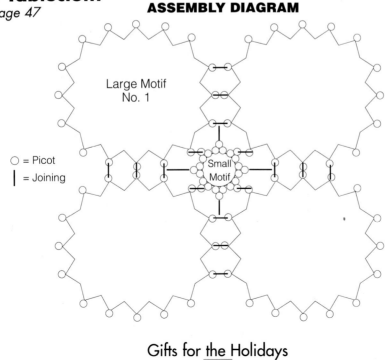

Large Motif No. 1

○ = Picot
| = Joining

Small Motif

Chapter Three

Holiday Fun

Any holiday mischief worth getting into requires at least one fellow conspirator. One to be the instigator, the other to act as backup. Crochet yourself the perfect holiday companion to add to your merrymaking and to the delight of family and friends.

Country Bunnies

Designed by Jocelyn Sass

VICTORIAN BUNNY

Finished Size

Bunny is 16" tall.

Materials

- ○ Worsted-weight yarn — 17 oz. white, small amount each slate blue and pale pink
- ○ Size 10 bedspread cotton — 150 yds. pink
- ○ 2 yds pink ¼" satin ribbon
- ○ Three pink ⅜" satin ribbon roses
- ○ (**Optional:** six small snaps)
- ○ Polyester fiberfill
- ○ Craft glue or hot glue gun
- ○ Tapestry needle
- ○ No. 6 steel and F crochet hooks or size needed to obtain gauge

Gauge

With **F hook,** 9 sc =2"; 9 sc rows = 2".

Notes: Do not join rnds unless otherwise stated. Mark first st of each rnd.

Use F hook and white unless otherwise stated.

Bunny
Head & Body

Rnd 1: Starting at **Head,** ch 2, 6 sc in 2nd ch from hook (6 sc).

Rnd 2: 2 sc in each st around.

Rnd 3: (Sc in next st, 2 sc in next st) around (18).

Rnd 4: (Sc in each of next 2 sts, 2 sc in next st) around (24).

Rnd 5: Sc in each st around.

Rnd 6: (Sc in each of next 3 sts, 2 sc in next st) around (30).

Rnd 7: (Sc in next 4 sts, 2 sc in next st) around (36).

Rnd 8: (Sc in next 5 sts, 2 sc in next st) around (42).

Rnds 9-14: Repeat rnd 5.

Rnd 15: Sc in first 18 sts; for **nose and cheek shaping,** 2 sc in each of next 6 sts; sc in last 18 sts.

Rnds 16-17: Repeat rnd 5.

Rnd 18: Sc in first 20 sts, (sc next 2 sts tog) 6 times, sc in each st around (42).

Rnd 19: (Sc in next 5 sts, sc next 2 sts tog) around (36).

Rnd 20: Repeat rnd 5.

Rnd 21: (Sc in next 4 sts, sc next 2 sts tog) around (30).

Rnd 22: Repeat rnd 5.

Rnd 23: (Sc in each of next 3 sts, sc next 2 sts tog) around (24).

Rnd 24: (Sc in each of next 2 sts, sc next 2 sts tog) around (18).

Rnd 25: Repeat rnd 5. Stuff.

Rnd 26: 2 sc in each st around (36).

Rnd 27: (Sc in next 5 sts, 2 sc in next st) around (42).

Rnd 28: (Sc in next 6 sts, 2 sc in next st) around (48).

Rnds 29-40: Repeat rnd 5.

Rnd 41: (Sc in next 6 sts, sc next 2 sts tog) around (42).

Rnd 42: Repeat rnd 5.

Rnd 43: Repeat rnd 19.

Rnd 44: Repeat rnd 5.

Rnd 45: (Sc in next 4 sts, sc next 2 sts tog) around (30).

Rnd 46: (Sc in each of next 3 sts, sc next 2 sts tog) around (24).

Rnd 47: (Sc in each of next 2 sts, sc next 2 sts tog) around (18). Stuff Body firmly.

Rnd 48: (Sc in next st, sc next 2 sts tog) around, join with sl st in first sc. Leaving 8" for sewing, fasten off (12). Sew opening closed.

Arm (make 2)

Rnds 1-3: Repeat same rnds of Head & Body.

Rnds 4-5: Sc in each st around.

Rnd 6: For **thumb shaping,** 2 sc in each of first 3 sts; sc in each st around (21).

Rnd 7: Repeat rnd 4.

Rnd 8: (Sc next 2 sts tog) 3 times, sc in each st around (18).

Rnd 9: (Sc next 2 sts tog) 2 times, sc in each st around (16).

Rnds 10-24: Repeat rnd 4. At end of last rnd, join with sl st in first sc.

Row 25: Working in rows, fold last rnd in half, working through both thicknesses, ch 1, sc in each st across leaving 8" for sewing, fasten off (8). Sew arms over rows 25-30 on each side of Body with thumbs pointing up.

Leg (make 2)

Rnd 1: Ch 10, sc in 2nd ch from hook, sc in each ch across with 3 sc in last ch; working on opposite side of ch, sc in each ch across with 2 sc in last ch (20).

Row 2: 2 sc in first st, sc in next

Continued on page 64

Country Bunnies

Continued from page 62

7 sts; for **toe shaping,** 2 hdc in each of next 3 sts; sc in next 7 sts, 2 sc in each of last 2 sts (26 sts).

Row 3: 2 sc in first st, sc in next 10 sts, 2 hdc in each of next 3 sts, sc in next 10 sts, 2 sc in each of last 2 sts (32 sts).

Rnd 4: Sc in each st around.

Rnd 5: Sc in first 12 sts, (sc next 2 sts tog) 3 times, sc in last 14 sts (29).

Rnd 6: Sc in first 11 sts, (dc next 2 sts tog) 3 times, sc in last 12 sts (26).

Rnd 7: Sc in first 10 sts, (dc next 2 sts tog) 3 times, sc in last 10 sts (23).

Rnd 8: Sc in each st around.

Rnd 9: Sc in first 9 sts; (dc next 2 sts tog) 3 times, sc in last 8 sts.

Rnds 10-14: Sc in each st around. Stuff foot firmly.

Rnds 15-30: Repeat row 10. At end of last rnd, join with sl st in first sc. Stuff.

Row 31: Repeat row 25 of Arm. Sew Legs to bottom of body ¼" apart.

Ear (make 2)

Rnds 1-4: Repeat same rnds of Head and Body.

Rnds 5-37: Sc in each st around. At end of last rnd, join with sl st in first sc.

Row 38: Repeat row 25 of Arm. Flatten last rnd and fold in half, sew Ears to each side of Head over rnd 3.

With slate blue, using Satin Stitch (see page159), embroider **eyes** over rnds 12 and 13 of Head 1¾" apart; with pale pink, embroider nose over rnds 16 and 17 centered below eyes.

Dress

Row 1: Ch 28, sc in 2nd ch from hook, sc in next 4 chs, (3 sc in next ch, sc in each of next 3 chs, 3 sc in next ch), sc in next 7 chs; repeat between ( ), sc in last 5 chs, turn (35 sc).

Row 2: Ch 1, sc in first 5 sts, *(2 sc in next st, 3 sc in next st, 2 sc in next st), sc in each of next 3 sts; repeat between ( )*, sc in next 7 sts; repeat between **, sc in last 5 sts, turn (51). Front of row 2 is right side of work.

Row 3: Ch 1, sc in first 8 sts, (3 sc in next st; for **sleeve ruffle,** 3 dc in each of next 9 sts; 3 sc in next st), sc in next 13 sts; repeat between ( ), sc in last 8 sts, turn (54 dc, 41 sc).

Row 4: Ch 1, sc in first 9 sts, (3 sc in next st, sc in next st, dc in next 27 sts, sc in next st, 3 sc in next st), sc in next 15 sts; repeat between ( ), sc in last 9 sts, turn (54 dc, 49 sc).

Rnd 5: Ch 1, sc in first 10 sts, (3 sc in next st, sc in each of next 2 sts, dc in next 27 sts, sc in each of next 2 sts, 3 sc in next st), sc in next 17 sts; repeat between ( ), sc in last 10 sts, turn (57 sc, 54 dc).

Row 6: Ch 1, sc in first 11 sts (3 sc in next st, sc in each of next 3 sts, dc in next 27 sts, sc in each of next 3 sts, 3 sc in next st), sc in next 19 sts; repeat between ( ), sc in last 11 sts, turn (65 sc, 54 dc).

Row 7: Ch 1, sc in first 13 sts; (for **armhole,** ch 4, skip next 35 sts); sc in next 23 sts; repeat between ( ), sc in last 13 sts, turn (49 sc, 2 ch-4 sps).

Row 8: Ch 1, sc in each sc and in each ch across, turn (57).

Row 9: Ch 1, sc in each st across, turn.

Row 10: Ch 1, sc in first st, (ch 1, skip next st, sc in next st) across, turn (29 sc, 28 ch-1 sps).

Row 11: Ch 3, 2 dc in same st, 3 dc in each ch-1 sp and in each sc across, turn (171).

Rows 12-15: Ch 3, dc in each st across, turn.

Row 16: Working this row in **back lps,** ch 3, dc in each st across, turn.

Rows 17-21: Repeat row 12.

Rows 22: Repeat row 16.

Row 23: Working this row in **front lps,** ch 3, dc in each st across, turn.

Row 24-28: Repeat row 12. At end of last row, fasten off.

Lower Ruffle

Row 1: Working in **back lps** of row 22, join with sl st in first st, ch 3, dc in each st across, turn (171 dc).

Rows 2-3: Ch 3, dc in each st across, turn. At end of last row, fasten off.

For **dress edging,** with right side of dress facing you, join with sc in end of row 1, sc in end of reach row on back edges and in each st across bottom of dress to opposite side of row 1 with 3 sc in each corner and working through both thicknesses on Lower Ruffle.

Sew center back seam.

(**Optional:** Sew snaps evenly spaced down back opening).

For **neck trim,** working in starting ch on opposite side of row 1, with No. 6 steel hook and pink bedspread cotton, join with sc in first ch, 7 sc in same ch, (sc in next ch, 8 sc in next ch) across, fasten off.

For **sleeve trim,** working around one armhole, with No. 6 steel hook and pink bedspread cotton, join with sc in st at underarm, (6 sc in next st, sc in next st) around, join with sl st in first sc, fasten off. Repeat on other armhole.

For **skirt trim,** working in **front lps** of row 15, with No. 6 steel hook and pink bedspread cotton, join with sc in first st, 5 sc in same st, (sc in next st, 6 sc in next st) across, fasten off. Repeat in remaining

front lps of row 21, in sts across bottom of Dress and across row 3 of Lower Ruffle. Weave 30" piece ribbon through ch sps of row 10, tie ends into a bow at front of Dress. Tie 12" piece ribbon into a bow, glue in front of one Ear. Glue one satin ribbon rose over center of each bow.

Purse

Rnd 1: Ch 4, sl st in first ch to form ring, ch 3, 11 dc in ring, join with sl st in top of ch-3 (12 dc).

Rnd 2: Ch 3, dc in same st, 2 dc in each st around, join (24).

Rnd 3: Ch 3, dc in each of next 2 sts, 2 dc in next st, (dc in each of next 3 sts, 2 dc in next st) around, join (30).

Rnds 4-8: Ch 3, dc in each st around, join.

Rnd 9: Ch 1, (sc in next st, ch 1, skip next st) around, join with sl st in first sc (15 ch sps).

Rnd 10: For **trim,** with No. 6 steel hook and pink bedspread cotton, join with sl st in any sc, ch 3, 5 dc in same st, sc in next ch sp, (6 dc in next sc, sc in next ch sp) around, join with sl st in top of ch-3, fasten off.

For **drawstring,** weave 12" piece ribbon through ch sps of rnd 9, pull tight and tie ends into a bow to secure. Glue satin ribbon rose over center of bow.

For **handle,** glue ends of 8" piece ribbon to each side of Purse on inside of rnd 9. Place handle over arm, glue to secure if desired.

BUNNY & BABY

Finished Size

Large bunny is 16" tall. Small bunny is 6" long.

Materials

○ Worsted-weight yarn — 7 ozs. off-white, 5 ozs. red, small amount each slate blue and pink
○ Straw hat with 5" head opening
○ Basket measuring 3" x 5"
○ 3 yds. red $\frac{7}{8}$" gingham ribbon
○ 2 yds off-white $\frac{1}{8}$" satin ribbon
○ 6" x 8" piece red cotton fabric
○ (**Optional:** six small snaps)
○ Craft glue or hot glue gun
○ Tapestry needle
○ F crochet hook or size needed to obtain gauge.

Gauge

9 sc =2"; 9 sc rows = 2".
Note: Do not join rnds unless otherwise stated. Mark first st of each rnd.

Large Bunny

With off-white, work same as Victorian Bunny's Head & Body, Arms, Legs and Ears. Work same eyes and nose using slate blue and pink.

Dress

Rows 1-8: With red, repeat same rows of Victorian Bunny's Dress.

Rows 9-13: Ch 1, sc in each st across, turn.

Row 14: Ch 1, 2 sc in each st across, turn (114).

Rows 15-33: Ch 1, sc in each st across, turn.

Row 34: For **ruffle,** ch 3, 2 dc in same st, 3 dc in each st across, turn (342).

Rows 35-36: Ch 3, dc in each st across, turn. At end of last row, **do not turn.**

Row 37: Ch 1, sc in end of each row and in each st

around to opposite end of row 36 with 3 sc in each corner at neck edge, fasten off. Sew center back seam (**Optional:** Sew snaps evenly spaced down back opening).

Sleeve Edgings

Rnd 1: Working around one armhole, join red with sc in any underarm st, sc in each st around, join with sl st in first sc.

Rnd 2: Ch 1, sc in each st around, join.

Rnd 3: Ch 1, sc in each of first 2 sts, ch 1, skip next st, (sc in next st, ch 1, skip next st) around, join, fasten off.
Repeat on other armhole.

Place dress on Bunny. For **each sleeve,** weave 18" piece $\frac{1}{8}$" ribbon through ch sps of rnd 3, tie in bow on top of Arm. Weave remaining $\frac{1}{8}$" ribbon through sts of row 13 on waist, tie ends into a bow at center front.

For **hat trim,** wrap 21" piece gingham ribbon around hat, cross ends in back leaving ends long, glue to secure. For **bow,** cut 3 pieces gingham ribbon each 12" long. For **each loop,** brings ends to center, glue to secure. Holding all 3 loops together, wrap separate 3" piece gingham ribbon around center of all loops, over lap and glue ends to secure. Glue bow over crossed ribbon ends on back of hat.

For **ties,** cut 36" piece gingham ribbon in half, glue one end of each piece inside hat on each side. Place hat on Bunny, tie into a bow under chin.

Baby Bunny
Head & Body

Rnds 1-3: With off-white repeat same rnds of Victorian Bunny's Head & Body.

Continued on page 81

Tissue Covers

Designed by Beverly Mewhorter

SPIDER TISSUE COVER

Size

Fits over boutique-style tissue box.

Materials

- ❍ Worsted-weight yarn —
  2 oz. orange and small
  amount black
- ❍ 5 black 12" chenille stems
- ❍ 10 round 6-mm wiggle eyes
- ❍ Craft glue or hot glue gun
- ❍ Tapestry needle
- ❍ H crochet hook or size
  needed to obtain gauge

Gauge

7 sc = 2"; 7 sc rows = 2"; 3 dc
rows and 3 sc rows = 2 ½".

Cover
Side (make 4)

Row 1: With orange, ch 20, sc
in 2nd ch from hook, (ch 2,
skip next 2 chs, sc in next ch)
across, turn (7 sc, 6 ch-2 sps).

Row 2: Ch 3, dc in same st, 3
dc in each sc across to last sc,
2 dc in last sc, turn (19 dc).

Row 3: Ch 1, sc in first st, (ch
2, skip next 2 sts, sc in next st)
across, turn (7 sc, 6 ch-2 sps).

Rows 4-12: Repeat rows 2

and 3 alternately, ending
with row 2. At end of last
row, fasten off.

Sew ends of rows on each
Side together.

Top

Row 1: With orange, ch 17, sc
in 2nd ch from hook, sc in
each ch across, turn (16 sc).

Rows 2-7: Ch 1, sc in each st
across, turn.

Row 8: Ch 1, sc in first 4 sts,
for **opening,** ch 8, skip next
8 sts; sc in last 4 sts, turn (8
sc, 1 ch-8 sp).

Row 9: Ch 1, sc in each st and
in each ch across, turn (16 sc).

Rows 10-15: Ch 1, sc in each st across, turn. At end of last row, fasten off.
Easing to fit, sew Top to last row of Sides.

Spider (make 5)
Rnd 1: For **body,** with black, ch 4, 9 dc in 4th ch from hook, join with sl st in top of ch-3 (10 dc).
Row 2: For **head,** sc in first st, dc in each of next 2 sts, (sc, sl st) in next st leaving remaining sts unworked, fasten off.

Finishing
1: Glue 2 eyes to center of Head on each Spider ⅛" apart.
2: For **legs,** cut 8 pieces of chenille stem each 1½" long. Bend each piece according to Leg Diagram. Glue 4 legs to each side of one Spider according to photo.
Repeat on other Spiders.
3: Glue one Spider at an angle over each Side and remaining Spider over corner of Top.

LEG DIAGRAM

TURKEY TISSUE COVER

Size

Fits over boutique-style tissue box.

Materials

○ Worsted-weight yarn — 2 oz. beige and small amount each brown, orange, red, and yellow
○ 2 round 8-mm wiggle eyes
○ Craft glue or hot glue gun
○ Tapestry needle
○ H crochet hook or size needed to obtain gauge

Gauge

7 sc = 2"; 2 dc rows and 2 sc rows = 1½".

Cover
Row 1: Starting at **sides,** with beige, ch 65, sl st in first ch to form ring, ch 1, sc in each ch around, join with sl st in first sc (65 sc).
Row 2: Ch 3, dc in each st around, join with sl st in top of ch-3.
Row 3: Ch 1, sc in each st around, join with sl st in first sc.
Rows 4-14: Repeat rnds 2 and 3 alternately, ending with rnd 2.
Row 15: Working in rows; for top, ch 1, sc in first 16 sts leaving remaining sts unworked, turn (16 sc).
Row 16: Ch 3, dc in each st across, turn.
Row 17: Ch 1, sc in each st across, turn.
Rows 18-19: Repeat rows 16 and 17.
Row 20: Ch 3, dc in each of next 3 sts; for **opening,** ch 8, skip next 8 sts; dc in last 4 sts, turn (8 dc, 1 ch-8 sp).
Row 21: Ch 1, sc in each st and in each ch across, turn (16 sc).
Rows 22-25: Repeat rows 16 and 17 alternately. At end of last row, fasten off.
Sew top to remaining sides.

Turkey
Body
Rnd 1: With brown, ch 4, 9 dc in 4th ch from hook, join with sl st in top of ch-3 (10 dc).
Rnd 2: Ch 3, dc in same st, 2 dc in each st around, join, fasten off.

Head
Repeat rnd 1 of Body, fasten off.

Long Feather (make 2 each yellow, red and orange)
Ch 8, sc in 2nd ch from hook, sc in next 5 chs, 2 sc in last ch; working on opposite side of ch, sc in each ch across, join with sl st in first sc, fasten off.

Short Feather (make one each red and yellow)
Ch 6, sc in 2nd ch form hook, sc in each ch across, fasten off.

Comb
With red, ch 3, sc in 2nd ch from hook, ch 1, (sc, sl st) in last ch, fasten off.
Sew Comb to top of Head.

Wattle
With red, ch 4, sl st in 2nd ch from hook, sl st in each ch across, fasten off.
Sew one end to center of Head.

Beak
With orange, ch 2, sl st in 2nd ch from hook, Fasten off.
Sew to center of Head above Wattle.

Foot (make 2)
With orange, ch 6, sl st in 2nd ch from hook, sl st in each of next 2 chs, (ch 4, sl st in 2nd ch from hook, sl st in each of next 2 chs) 2 times, sl st in each of last 2 chs of first ch-6, fasten off.

Finishing
1: Glue bottom half of Head to top of rnd 2 on Body.
2: Glue Body, Tail Feathers, Wings and Feet to one side of Cover as shown in photo.
3: Glue wiggle eyes to center of Head above Beak ⅛" apart. •

Lucky Leprechaun

Designed by Noelle Goetz

Finished Size

Leprechaun is 14½" tall.

Materials

- ⃝ Worsted-weight yarn — 2 oz. dk. green, 1 oz. each mint green and peach, small amount each rust, black and gold
- ⃝ Dk. peach embroidery floss
- ⃝ Two ½ animal eyes with washers
- ⃝ Polyester fiberfill
- ⃝ Tapestry needle
- ⃝ G crochet hook or size needed to obtain gauge

Gauge

4 sc sts = 1"; 4 sc rows = 1".

Head & Body

Note: Do not join rnds unless otherwise stated. Mark first st of each rnd.

Rnd 1: Starting at **Head,** with peach, ch 2, 6 sc in 2nd ch from hook (6 sc).

Rnd 2: 2 sc in each st around (12).

Rnd 3: (Sc in next st, 2 sc in next st) around (18).

Rnd 4: (Sc in each of next 2 sts, 2 sc in next st) around (24).

Rnd 5: (Sc in each of next 3 sts, 2 sc in next st) around (30).

Rnd 6: Sc in first st, (2 sc in next st, sc in next 4 sts) 5 times, 2 sc in next st, sc in each of last 3 sts (36).

Rnds 7-9: Sc in each st around (36).

Rnd 10: Sc in first 17 sts; **for nose shaping,** 2 sc in each of next 2 sts; sc in last 17 sts (38).

Rnd 11: Sc in first 13 sts; **for cheek shaping,** 2 sc in each of next 3 sts; sc in each of next 2 sts, 2 sc in each of next 2 sts, sc in each of next 2 sts; for **cheek shaping,** 2 sc in each of next 3 sts; sc in last 13 sts (46).

Rnd 12: Sc in first 21 sts, (sc next 2 sts tog) 2 times, sc in last 21 sts (44).

Rnd 13: Sc in first 20 sts, (sc next 2 sts tog) 2 times, sc in last 20 sts (42).

Rnd 14: Sc in first 12 sts, (sc next 2 sts tog) 3 times, sc in next st; for **chin shaping,** 2 sc in each of next 4 sts; sc in next st, (sc next 2 sts tog) 3 times, sc in last 12 sts (40).

Rnd 15: Sc in each st around.

Rnd 16: Sc in first st, sc next 2 sts tog, (sc in each of next 3 sts, sc next 2 sts tog) 3 times, (sc next 2 sts tog) 2 times, (sc next 2 sts tog, sc in each of next 3 sts) 3 times, sc next 2 sts tog, sc in last st (30).

Rnd 17: (Sc in each of next 3 sts, sc next 2 sts tog) around (24).

Rnd 18: (Sc in each of next 2 sts, sc next 2 sts tog) around, join with sl st in first sc, fasten off (18).

Attach eyes ¾" apart centered above nose between rnds 9 and 10. Stuff Head.

Rnd 19: Join mint green with sc in first st, sc in same st, 2 sc in each st around, **do not join** (36).

Rnds 20-28: Sc in each st around. At end of last rnd, join with sl st in first sc, fasten off.

Rnd 29: Join dk. green with sc in first st, sc in each st around, **do not join.**

Rnds 30-37: Sc in each st around. At end of last rnd, join with sl st in first sc, fasten off. Stuff.

Flatten last rnd and sew closed.

Leg (make 2)

Rnd 1: Starting at **shoe,** ch 15, sc in 2nd ch from hook, sc in next 12 chs, 4 sc in last ch; working on opposite side of ch, sc in next 12 chs, 3 sc in last ch, join with sl st in first sc (32 sc).

Rnd 2: Ch 1, sc in each st around, join.

Rnd 3: Ch 1, sc in first 12 sts; for **toe,** (sc next 2 sts tog) 3 times; sc in last 14 sts, join (26).

Rnd 4: Ch 1, sc in first 11 sts, (sc next 2 sts tog) 3 times, sc in last 12 sts, join (26)

Rnd 5: Ch 1, sc in first 9 sts, (sc next 2 sts tog) 4 times, sc in last 9 sts, join (22).

Rnd 6: Ch 1, sc in first 7 sts, (sc next 2 sts tog) 4 times, sc in last 7 sts, join (18).

Rnd 7: Working this rnd in **front lps** only, ch 1, sc in each st around, join, fasten off.

Flatten toe and curl over top of shoe. Tack rows 3 and 5 together. Stuff.

Rnd 8: For **Leg,** working in **back lps** of rnd 6, join mint green with sc in first st, sc in each of next 3 sts, sc next 2 sts tog, (sc in next 4 sts, sc next 2 sts tog) around, join (15).

Rnd 9: Ch 1, sc in each st around, **do not join.**

Continued on page 72

Theodore Bear

Designed by Patricia Bryant

Finished Size

Bear is 16" tall.

Materials

- ○ Worsted-weight yarn — 6 oz. brown, 1 oz. off-white, small amount each dk. brown and red
- ○ Two 18-mm. animal eyes with washers
- ○ ½ yd. satin ribbon
- ○ Polyester fiberfill
- ○ Tapestry needle
- ○ H crochet hook or size needed to obtain gauge

Gauge

7 sc = 2"; 4 sc rows = 1".

Notes: All sc are worked in space between the two vertical bars (see illustration).

Do not join rnds unless otherwise stated. Mark first st of each rnd.

Use brown unless otherwise stated.

SC BETWEEN VERTICAL BARS

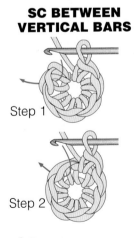

Step 1

Step 2

Head Front

Rnd 1: Ch 2, 6 sc in 2nd ch from hook (6 sc).

Rnd 2: 2 sc in each st around (12).

Rnd 3: (Sc in next st, 2 sc in next st) around (18).

Rnd 4: (Sc in each of next 2 sts, 2 sc in next st) around (24).

Rnd 5: (Sc in each of next 3 sts, 2 sc in next st) around (30).

Rnd 6: Sc in each st around.

Rnd 7: (Sc in next 4 sts, 2 sc in next st) around (36).

Rnd 8: (Sc in next 5 sts, 2 sc in next st) around (42).

Rnd 9: (Sc in next 6 sts, 2 sc in next st) around (48).

Rnd 10: (Sc in next 7 sts, 2 sc in next st) around (54).

Rnds 11-14: Sc in each st around. At end of last rnd, join with sl st in first sc, fasten off.

Attach eyes over rows 6 and 7 of Head 1½" apart.

Muzzle

Rnds 1-3: With off-white, repeat same rnds of Head Front.

Rnds 4-6: Sc in each st around. At end of last rnd, join with sl st in first sc, fasten off.

Lower Lip

Row 1: With off-white, ch 11, sc in 2nd ch from hook, sc in each ch across, turn (10 sc).

Row 2: Ch 1, sc in each st across, turn.

Row 3: Fold piece in half lengthwise; working through both thicknesses, sl st in each st across, fasten off.

For **inside of mouth,** with red, ch 6, sc in 2nd ch from hook, hdc in next ch, 3 dc in next ch, hdc in next ch, sc in last ch, fasten off.

Sew curved side to row 3 of Lower Lip. Sew Lower Lip and inside of mouth over 8 sts of rnd 6 on Muzzle.

Sew Muzzle to Head centered below eyes, stuffing before closing.

With dk. brown, using Satin Stitch (see page 159), embroider **nose** as shown in photo. For **noseline,** with dk.brown, make one long stitch under nose through rnds 1-6 of Muzzle, pull tight, secure.

Head Back

Rnds 1-5: Repeat same rnds of Head Front.

Rnds 6-9: Repeat rnds 7-10 of Head Front.

Rnd 10: Sc in each st around, join with sl st in first sc.

Rnd 11: Holding Front and Back wrong sides together, matching sts, sl st in each st around through **back lps,** stuffing before closing, join, fasten off.

Ear (make 2)

Rnds 1-3: Repeat same rnds of Head Front.

Rnds 4-7: Sc in each st around.

Rnd 8: (Sc in next st, sc next 2 sts tog) around, join with sl st in first sc, fasten off (12).

Flatten last rnd; sew to top of Head 2½" apart.

Body

Rnd 1: Starting at **neck edge,** ch 18, sl st in first ch to form ring, ch 1, sc in each ch around (18 sc).

Rnd 2: (Sc in each of next 2 sts, 2 sc in next 2 st) around (24).

Continued on page 72

Theodore Bear

Continued from page 71

Rnd 3: (Sc in each of next 3 sts, 2 sc in next st) around (30).
Rnd 4: Sc in each st around.
Rnd 5: (Sc in next 4 sts, 2 sc in next st) around (36).
Rnd 6: Sc in each st around.
Rnd 7: (Sc in next 5 sts, 2 sc in next st) around (42).
Rnds 8-11: Sc in each st around.
Rnd 12: (Sc in next 6 sts, 2 sc in next st) around (48).
Rnd 13: (Sc in next 7 sts, 2 sc in next st) around (54).
Rnds 14-19: Sc in each st around.
Rnd 20: (Sc in next 7 sts, sc next 2 sts tog) around (48).
Rnd 21: (Sc in next 6 sts, sc next 2 sts tog) around (42).
Rnd 22: (Sc in next 5 sts, sc next 2 sts tog) around (36).
Row 23: Sc in each st around.
Row 24: (Sc in next 4 sts, sc next 2 sts tog) around (30).
Rnds 25-26: Sc in each st around. At end of last rnd, join sl st in first sc. Stuff.
Rnd 27: Flatten last rnd; working through both thicknesses, sl st in each st across, fasten off.

Tummy Patch

Rnds 1-10: With off-white, repeat same rnds of Head Front. At end of last rnd, fasten off.
Center and sew over front of Body, slightly stuffing before closing. Sew Head to Body.

Arm (make 2)

Rnds 1-3: Repeat same rnds of Head Front.
Rnds 4-6: Sc in each st around.
Rnd 7: For wrist shaping, (sc in next st, sc next 2 sts tog) around (12).
Rnds 8-9: Sc in each st around.
Rnd 10: (Sc in next st, 2 sc in next st) around (18).
Rnds 11-20: Sc in each st around.
Rnd 21: (Sc next 2 sts tog, sc in next 7 sts) around (16).
Rnd 22: (Sc next 2 sts tog, sc in next 6 sts) around (14).
Rnd 23: (Sc next 2 sts tog, sc in next 5 sts) around, join with sl st in first sc, fasten off (12). Stuff.
Flatten last rnd; sew over rnds 3-7 on each side of Body.

Leg (make 2)

Rnd 1: Ch 20, sl st in first ch to form ring, ch 1, sc in each ch around (20 sc).
Rnds 2-11: Sc in each st around.
Rnds 12-15: For ankle shaping, sl st in first 10 sts, sc in last 10 sts.
Rnd 16-22: Sc in each st around. At end of last rnd, join with sl st in first sc.
Row 23: Flatten last rnd; working through both thicknesses, sc in each st across, turn (10).
Note: For **puff st,** yo, insert hook in next st, draw up long lp, (yo, insert hook in same st, yo, draw up long lp) 2 times, yo, draw through all 7 lps on hook.
Row 24: For **toes,** ch 2, puff st, ch 2, (sl st in next st, ch 2, puff st, ch 2) across, sl st in same st as last st made, fasten off (5 puff sts). Stuff.
Flatten rnd 1; working through both thicknesses on opposite side of starting ch, join with sc in first ch, sc in each ch across, fasten off. Sew Legs to bottom of Body. Tie ribbon into a bow around neck. •

Lucky Leprechaun

Continued from page 68

Rnds 10-14: Sc in each st around. At end of last rnd, join with sl st in first sc, fasten off.
Rnd 15: Join dk. green with sc in first st, sc in each of next 3 sts, 2 sc in next st, (sc in next 4 sts, 2 sc in next st) around, **do not join** (18).
Rnds 16-20: Sc in each st around. At end of last rnd, join with sl st in first sc, fasten off. Stuff.
Flatten last rnd and sew Legs to bottom of Body.

Right Arm

Rnd 1: Starting at **hand,** with peach, ch 2, 6 sc in 2nd ch from hook (6 sc).
Rnd 2: 2 st in each st around (12).
Rnds 3-4: Sc in each st around.
Rnd 5: For **thumb,** ch 6, sc in 2nd ch from hook, sc in last 4 chs, sc in each st around (17).
Rnd 6: Working behind thumb, sc in each st around (12).
Rnd 7: (Sc in each of next 2 sts, sc next 2 sts tog) around (9).
Rnd 8: Sc in each st around, join with sl st in first sc, fasten off.
Rnd 9: Join mint green with sc in first st, sc in next st, 2 sc in next st, (sc in each of next 2 sts, 2 sc in next st) around, **do not join** (12).
Rnd 10: Sc in each st around.
Rnd 11: (Sc in each of next 3 sts, 2 sc in next st) around (15).
Rnds 12-19: Sc in each st around.
Rnd 20: Hdc in first st; for **shoulder,** dc in next 7 sts; hdc in next st, sc in last 6 sts, join with sl st in top of first hdc, fasten off. Stuff.
With thumb toward front, flatten last rnd and sew to rnd 21 on right side of Body.

Left Arm

Rnds 1-19: Repeat same rnds of Right Arm. At end of last rnd, join with sl st in first sc.
Rnd 20: For **shoulder,** ch 3, dc in each of next 2 sts; hdc in next st, sc in next 6 sts, hdc in next st; for **shoulder,** dc in last 4 sts; join with sl st in top of ch-3, fasten off. Stuff.

With thumb toward front, flatten last rnd and sew to rnd 21 on left side of Body.

Hat

Rnds 1-6: With dk. green, repeat same rnds of Head & Body.

Rnd 7: (Sc in next 5 sts, 2 sc in next st) around, join with sl st in first sc (42).

Rnd 8: Working this rnd in **back lps** only, ch 1 sc in each st around, join.

Rnd 9: Ch 1, sc in each st around, join.

Rnd 10: Ch 1, (sc in next 5 sts, sc next 2 sts tog) around, join, fasten off (36).

Rnd 11: Join black with sc in first st, sc in each st around, join.

Rnds 12-13: Ch 1, sc in each st around, join. At end of last rnd, fasten off.

Rnd 14: Working this rnd in **front lps** only, join dk. green with sc in first st, sc in next 4 sts, 2 sc in next st, (sc in next 5 sts, 2 sc in next st) around, join (42).

Rnd 15: Ch 1, sc in first 6 sts, 2 sc in next st, (sc in next 6 sts, 2 sc in next st) around, join (48).

Rnd 16: Ch 1, sc in first 7 sts, 2 sc in next st, (sc in next 7 sts, 2 sc in next st) around, join (54).

Rnd 17: Ch 1, sc in first 8 sts, 2 sc in next st, (sc in next 8 sts, 2 sc in next st) around, join, fasten off (60).

For **buckle,** with gold, ch 16, sl st in first ch, fasten off.

Shape into a square and sew over rnds 10-13 on front of Hat.

Vest Side (make 2)

Row 1: With dk. green, ch 8, sc in 2nd ch from hook, sc in each ch across, turn (7 sc).

Rows 2-4: Ch 1, 2 sc in first st, sc in each st across with 2 sc in last st, turn (9, 11, 13).

Row 5: Ch 1, sc in each st across, turn.

Row 6: Ch 1, 2 sc in first st, sc in next 6 sts, sc next 2 sts tog leaving remaining sts unworked, turn (9).

Row 7: Repeat row 5.

Row 8: Ch 1, 2 sc in first st, sc in each st across, turn (10).

Rows 9-13: Repeat rows 5 and 8 alternately, ending with row 5 and 12 sts in last row.

Row 14: Ch 1, 2 sc in first st, sc in next 10 sts, 2 sc in last st; for **armhole,** ch 8, skip next unworked st on row 5; sl st in each of last 3 sts on row 5, turn (17 sts, 8 chs).

Row 15: Skip first 3 sl sts, dc in next ch, hdc in next ch, sc in each of next 2 chs, hdc in next ch, dc in next ch, ch 1, 2 sc around side of dc just made, sc in each of last 2 chs, sc in each st across row 14, turn (24 sts).

Row 16: Ch 1, 2 sc in first st, sc in next 17 sts leaving remaining sts unworked, turn (19 sc).

Rows 17-20: Repeat rows 5 and 8 alternately, ending with 21 sts in last row. At end of last row, fasten off

Holding 2 Sides together, starting at neckline, sew 10 sts of last row, together.

For **vest trim,** join dk. green with sl st in any st, ch 1; working left to right, **reverse sc** (see page 159) in each st and in end of each row around, join with sl st in first sc, fasten off.

For **armhole trim;** working around one armhole, join dk. green with sl st at underarm, ch 1, reverse sc in each st around, join with sl st in first sc, fasten off.

Repeat on other armhole. Place Vest on doll.

Bow Tie

Row 1: With black, ch 4, sc in 2nd ch from hook, sc in each of last 2 chs, turn (3 sc).

Rows 2-8: Ch 1, sc in each st across, turn. At end of last row, fasten off.

Cut 24" strand black, wrap around middle of Tie 5 times, tie in knot to secure. Tie Bow Tie around neck.

Hair

Cut 130 pieces rust yarn each 5" long. For **each hair fringe,** fold one piece of yarn in half, insert hook in st, draw fold through, draw all loose ends through fold, tighten. Trim ends.

Fringe around face to back of Head as shown in photo.

Finishing

1: Stuff Hat lightly wth small amount of fiberfill. With dk. green, tack Hat to top of Head.

2: With tapestry needle and peach yarn, solf-sculpture face by making small stitches to draw eyes closer together. Make stitches above and below nose and on each side of chin.

3: With 2 strands dk. peach embroidery floss, using Outline Stitch (see page 159), embroider **mouth** across rnd 13 on front of Head as shown in photo.

4: Fold thumb in half towards shoulder. With peach thread, sew thumb layers together.

5: For shoe buckles, separate 2 ply from a 12" piece of gold yarn. Using Straight Stitch (see page 159), embroider a small square over rnds 5 and 6 of each Shoe. •

Easter Bonnet Chick

Designed by Michele Wilcox

Finished Size

Chick is 10" tall sitting.

Materials

- ○ Worsted-weight yarn — 4 oz. gold, 2 oz. peach and small amount each black, blue, green and purple
- ○ Straw hat with 4" head opening
- ○ Polyester fiberfill
- ○ Craft glue or hot glue gun
- ○ Tapestry needle
- ○ K crochet hook or size needed to obtain gauge

Gauge

With **2 strands yarn held tog,** 5 sc sts = 2"; 5 sc rows = 2".

Notes: Do not join rnds unless otherwise stated. Mark first st of each rnd.

Work entire pattern with 2 strands yarn held together.

Head & Body

Rnd 1: Starting at **Head,** with gold, ch 2, 6 sc in 2nd ch from hook (6 sc).

Rnd 2: 2 sc in each st around (12).

Rnd 3: (Sc in next st, 2 sc in next st) around (18).

Rnd 4: (Sc in each of next 2 sts, 2 sc in next st) around (24).

Rnd 5: (Sc in each of next 3 sts, 2 sc in next st) around (30).

Rnd 6: Sc in each st around.

Rnd 7: (Sc in next 4 sts, 2 sc in next st) around (36).

Rnds 8-9: Sc in each st around.

Rnd 10: (Sc in next 4 sts, next 2 sts tog) around (30).

Rnds 11-13: Sc in each st around.

Rnd 14: (Sc next 2 sts tog) around (15).

Rnd 15: Sc in each st around. Stuff. Continue stuffing as you work.

Rnd 16: 2 sc in each st around (30).

Rnd 17: (Sc in next 4 sts, 2 sc in next st) around (36).

Rnd 18: Sc in each st around.

Rnd 19: (Sc in next 5 sts, 2 sc in next st) around (42).

Rnds 20-28: Sc in each st around.

Rnd 29: (Sc in next 5 sts, sc next 2 sts tog) around (36).

Rnd 30: (Sc in next 4 sts, sc next 2 sts tog) around (30).

Rnd 31: (Sc in each of next 3 sts, sc next 2 sts tog) around (24).

Rnd 32: (Sc next 2 sts tog) around, join with sl st in first sc, fasten off (12). Sew opening closed.

With black, using Satin Stitch (see page 159), embroider eyes 2¼" apart over rnd 7 as shown in photo.

Wing (make 2)

Rnds 1-2: Repeat same rnds of Head & Body.

Rnd 3: Sc in each st around.

Rnd 4: (Sc in next st, 2 sc in next st) around (18).

Rnds 5-7: Sc in each st around.

Rnd 8: (Sc in next st, sc next 2 sts tog) around, join with sl st in first sc, fasten off (12).

Flatten last rnd and sew over rnds 18-23 on each side of Body.

Beak Side (Make 2)

Rnd 1: With peach, ch 2, 6 sc in 2nd ch from hook (6 sc).

Rnd 2: (Sc in next st, 2 sc in next st) around (9).

Rnd 3: Sc in each st around, join with sl st in first sc, fasten off.

Flatten last rnd and sew first Beak Side to rnd 9 centered below eyes. Sew 2nd Beak Side directly under first Beak Side.

Leg (make 2)

Rnd 1: With peach, ch 2, 6 sc in 2nd ch from hook (6 sc).

Rnds 2-7: Sc in each st around. At end of last rnd, join with sl st in first sc, fasten off.

Toe (make 6)

Rnd 1: With peach, ch 2, 6 sc in 2nd ch from hook (6 sc).

Rnds 2-4: Sc in each st around. At end of last rnd, join with sl st in first sc, fasten off.

Sew 3 Toes to bottom of each Leg. Sew Legs 3½" apart to rnds 27-28 on front of Body.

Flower (make 2 gold/purple, make 2 gold/blue)

Rnd 1: With gold, ch 2, 6 sc in 2nd ch from hook, join with sl st in first sc, fasten off (6 sc).

Rnd 2: Join flower color with sl st in any st, ch 3, (sl st in next st, ch 3) around, join with sl st in first sl st, fasten off.

Leaf (make 2)

With green, ch 4, sc in 2nd ch from hook, sc in next ch, 3 sc in last ch; working on opposite side of ch, sc in next ch, 2 sc in last ch, join with sl st in first sc, fasten off.

Glue Flowers and Leaves to hat as desired. •

Pilgrim Turkey

Designed by Estella Whitford

Finished Size

Turkey is 9½" tall when sitting.

Materials

- ○ Worsted-weight yarn — 3½ oz. brown, 2 oz. rust, 1 oz. each black, burgundy, gold, green, lavender, purple, tan and white
- ○ Two black 12-mm. eyes with washers
- ○ 12" white ⅝" satin ribbon
- ○ 12" black ⅝" satin ribbon
- ○ Polyester fiberfill
- ○ Tapestry needle
- ○ G crochet hook or size needed to obtain gauge

Gauge

4 sc sts = 1"; 4 sc rows = 1".

Note: Do not join rnds unless otherwise stated. Mark first st of each rnd.

Head & Body Side (make 2)

Row 1: Starting at **Head,** with brown, ch 8, sc in 2nd ch from hook, sc in each ch across, turn (7 sc).

Rows 2-4: Ch 1, 2 sc in first st, sc in each st across with 2 sc in last st, turn, ending with 13 sts in last row.

Rows 5-10: Ch 1, sc in each st across, turn. Attach eyes ½" apart over rnds 5 and 6.

Row 11: Ch 1, sc first 2 sts tog, sc in each st across to last 2 sts, sc last 2 sts tog, turn (11).

Row 12: Ch 1, sc in each st across, turn.

Rows 13-14: Repeat rows 11 and 12, ending with 9 sts in last row.

Rows 15-18: Repeat row 2, ending with 17 sts in last row.

Rows 19-26: Ch 1, sc in each st across, turn.

Rows 27-30: Repeat row 11, ending with 9 sts in last row.

Rnd 31: Working around entire outer edge, ch 1, sc in each st and in end of each row around, join with sl st in first sc, fasten off. Sew Head & Body sides together, stuffing before closing.

Arm (make 2)

Rnd 1: With brown, ch 2, 6 sc in 2nd ch from hook (6 sc).

Rnd 2: 2 sc in each st around (12).

Rnd 3: (Sc in next st, 2 sc in next st) around (18).

Rnds 4-6: Sc in each st around.

Rnd 7: (Sc in next st, sc next 2 sts tog) around (12).

Rnds 8-12: Sc in each st around. At end of last rnd, join with sl st in first sc. Leaving 8" for sewing, fasten off.

Flatten Arms and sew over rows 17-20 on each side of Body.

Leg (make 2)

Rnd 1: With rust, ch 2, 6 sc in 2nd ch from hook (6 sc).

Rnd 2: (Sc in each of next 2 sts, 2 sc in next st) around (8).

Rnds 3-18: Sc in each st around, stuffing as you work. At end of last rnd, join with sl st in first sc. Leaving 8" for sewing, fasten off.

Foot Side (make 4)

Rnds 1-3: Repeat same rnds of Arm.

Rnd 4: For **toes,** *(hdc, dc) in next st, (tr, dc, sc) in next st; repeat from * 2 more times, sl st in next st leaving remaining sts unworked. Leaving 8" for sewing, fasten off.

For **each Foot,** holding 2 Sides wrong sides together, matching sts, sew together. Sew last rnd of one Leg over rnds 1-3 on back of each Foot. Sew Legs to front of Body ½" apart over rows 27 and 28 as shown in photo.

Beak

Rnd 1: With rust, ch 2, 6 sc in 2nd ch from hook (6 sc).

Rnd 2: (Sc in each of next 2 sts, 2 sc in next st) around (8).

Rnds 3-4: (Sc in next st, 2 sc in next st) around (12, 18).

Rnd 5: Sc in each st around, join with sl st in first sc. Leaving 8" for sewing, fasten off.

Flatten and sew over rnds 7-9 on Front of Head as shown.

For **wattle,** with burgundy, ch 12, sl st in first ch, fasten off. Sew centered below Beak as shown.

Collar

Row 1: With white, ch 30, sc in 2nd ch from hook, sc in each ch across, turn (29 sc).

Row 2: Ch 1, 2 sc in first st, sc in each st across with 2 sc in last st, turn (31).

Continued on page 80

Pumpkin Patch Pillow

Designed by Michele Wilcox

Finished Size

Pillow is 11" x 12".

Materials

○ Worsted-weight yarn — 3½ oz. med green, 2½ oz. peach, 1 oz. black, small amount each brown and dk. green
○ Small amount dk. green size 3 pearl cotton
○ Polyester fiberfill
○ Tapestry needle
○ No. 2 steel, F and H crochet hooks or sizes needed to obtain gauges

Gauges

With **F hook and worsted-weight,** 9 sc = 2"; 9 sc rows = 2". **With H hook and worsted-weight,** 7 hdc = 2"; 5 hdc rows = 2".

Pillow
Side (make 2)

Row 1: With H hook and med. green, ch 36, hdc in 3rd ch from hook, hdc in each ch across, turn (35 hdc).

Rows 2-26: Ch 2, hdc in each st across turn. At end of last row, for **first Side,** fasten off; for **2nd Side, do not fasten off.**

Edging

Rnd 1: Holding Sides wrong sides together, matching sts and working through both thicknesses, ch 1, 3 sc in first st, sc in each st across to last st, 3 sc in last st; *working in ends of rows, skip first row, sc in next row, (2 sc in next row, sc in next row) across*; working in starting ch on opposite side of row 1, 3 sc in first ch, sc in each ch across to last ch, 3 sc in last ch; repeat between ** stuffing before closing, join with sl st in first sc, fasten off (152 sc).

Rnd 2: Join black with sl st in any center corner st, ch 3, 4 dc in same st, skip next st, sc in next st, skip next st, (5 dc in next st, skip next st, sc in next st, skip next st) around, join with sl st in top of ch 3, fasten off.

Long Pumpkin

Row 1: With F hook and peach, ch 8, 2 sc in 2nd ch from hook, sc in each ch across to last ch, 2 sc in last ch, turn (9 sc).

Rows 2-3: Ch 1, 2 sc in first st, sc in each st across to last st, 2 sc in last st, turn (11, 13).

Rows 4-22: Ch 1, sc in each st across, turn.

Rows 23-27: Ch 1, sc first 2 sts tog, sc in each st across to last 2 sts, sc last 2 sts tog, turn, ending with 3 sc in last row. At end of last row, fasten off.

Row 28: For **stem,** join brown with sc in first st, sc in each of last 2 sts, turn.

Rows 20-33: Ch 1, sc in each st across, turn.

Row 34: Ch 1, 2 sc in first st, sc in each st across, fasten off (4).

Finishing

1: With black, using Satin Stitch (see page 159), embroider eyes 1" apart over rows 20 and 21 as shown in photo.

2: With black, using Satin Stitch, embroider nose centered below eyes over rows 16 and 17 as shown.

3: With black, using Satin Stitch, embroider **mouth** centered below nose over rows 9-13 as shown.

4: Sew pumpkin horizontally over rows 4-11 on Pillow front as shown, stuffing lightly before closing.

Medium Pumpkin

Row 1: With F hook and peach, ch 11, 2 sc in 2nd ch from hook, sc in each ch across to last ch, 2 sc in last ch, turn (12 sc).

Rows 2-4: Ch 1, 2 sc in first st, sc in each st across to last st, 2 sc in last st turn (14, 16, 18).

Rows 5-13: Ch 1 sc in each st across, turn.

Rows 14-15: Ch 1, sc first 2 sts tog, sc in each st across to last 2 sts, sc last 2 sts tog, turn (16, 14). At end of last row, fasten off.

Row 16: Skip first 5 sts; for

Continued on page 80

Pumpkin Patch Pillow

Continued from page 79

stem, join brown with sc in next st, sc in each of next 3 sts leaving remaining sts unworked, turn (4).

Rows 17-18: Ch 1, sc in each st across, turn. At end of last row, fasten off.

Finishing

1: With black, using Satin Stitch, embroider eyes ¾" apart over rows 9 and 10 as shown in photo.

2: With black, using Satin Stitch, embroider **nose** centered below eyes over row 7 as shown.

3: With black, using Satin Stitch, embroider **mouth** centered below nose over rows 4 and 5 as shown.

4: Sew pumpkin horizontally over rows 14-24 on Pillow front as shown, stuffing lightly before closing.

Small Pumpkin

Row 1: With F hook and peach, ch 8, 2 sc in 2nd ch from hook, sc in each ch across to last ch, 2 sc in last ch, turn (9 sc).

Rows 2-9: Repeat same rows of Long Pumpkin.

Rows 10-11: Ch 1, sc first 2 sts tog, sc in each st across to last 2 sts, sc last 2 sts tog, turn

(11, 9). At end of last row, fasten off.

Row 12: Skip first 3 sts; for **stem,** join brown with sc in next st, sc in each of next 2 sts leaving remaining sts unworked, turn (3).

Rows 13-14: Ch 1 sc in each st across, turn. At end of last row, fasten off.

Finishing

1: With black, using Satin Stitch, embroider eyes ¾" apart over rows 7 and 8 as shown in photo.

2: With black, using Satin Stitch, embroider **mouth** centered below eyes over rows 3 and 4 as shown.

3: Sew Pumpkin at an angle above Medium Pumpkin as shown, stuffing lightly before closing.

Leaf

Rnd 1: With G hook and dk. green worsted-weight, ch 9, sc in 2nd ch from hook, hdc in next ch, dc in each of next 2 chs, tr in each of next 2 chs, dc in next ch, 5 hdc in last ch; working on opposite side of ch, dc in next ch, tr in each of next 2 chs, dc in each of next 2 chs, hdc in next ch, sc in last ch, join with sl st in first sc (19 sts).

Rnd 2: Ch 2, dc in same st, *sc in next st; ch 1, (dc, tr, ch 3, sl st) in next st*; repeat between ** 2 more times, sc in each of next 2 sts, (hdc, dc, ch 1, dc, hdc) in next st, sc in next st; repeat between ** 3 more times, sc in next st, ch 1, dc in last st, ch 2, join with sl st in same st as joining sl st on last rnd, fasten off.

Sew above Medium Pumpkin as shown.

Small Vine

With No. 2 steel hook and pearl cotton, ch 15, 3 sc in 2nd ch from hook, 3 sc in each ch across, fasten off.

Sew one end to row 1 of stem on Small Pumpkin as shown.

Medium Vine

With No. 2 steel hook and pearl cotton, ch 20, 3 sc in 2nd ch from hook, 3 sc in each ch across, fasten off.

Sew one end to row 1 of stem on Medium Pumpkin as shown.

Large Vine

With No. 2 steel hook and pearl cotton, ch 31, 3 sc in 2nd ch from hook, 3 sc in each ch across, fasten off.

Sew one end to row 1 of stem on Large Pumpkin as shown. •

Pilgrim Turkey

Continued from page 77

Row 3: Ch 1, sc in each st across, fasten off.

Row 4: Working in starting ch on opposite side of row 1, with right side facing you, join white with sc in first ch, sc in each ch across, turn.

Row 5: Ch 1, sc in each st across, fasten off.

Bib

Row 1: With white, ch 4, sc in 2nd ch from hook, sc in each ch across, turn (3 sc).

Rows 2-3: Ch 1, 2 sc in first st, sc in each st across with 2 sc in last st, turn (5, 7).

Row 4-6: Ch 1, sc in each st across, turn. At end of last row, **do not turn.**

Row 7: Ch 1, sc in next 6 rows; working in starting ch on opposite side of row 1, sc in next ch, (sc, ch 3, sc) in next ch, sc in next ch, sc in next 6 rows, sl st in first st of row 6. Leaving 8" for sewing, fasten off.

With black, using French Knot (see page 159), embroider 3 buttons down Bib ½" apart.

Place Collar around neck with row 3 facing up and ends meeting under Wattle. Sew ends of rows 4 and 5 of Collar together. Sew row 6 of Bib to row 5 of Collar on center front of Body.

Cut V-shape into each end of black ribbon; tie into bow around neck over Collar.

Hat
Rnds 1-3: Repeat same rnds of Arm on page 77.

Rnd 4: (Sc in each of next 2 sts, 2 sc in next st) around (24).

Rnd 5: Working this rnd in **back lps,** sc in each st around.

Rnds 6-10: Sc in each st around.

Rnd 11: Working this rnd in **front lps,** (sc in each of next 3 sts, 2 sc in next st) around (30).

Rnd 12: (Sc in next 4 sts, 2 sc in next st) around (36).

Rnd 13: (Sc in next 5 sts, 2 sc in next st) around, fasten off (42).

Place Hat over rows 1-3 of Head, stuff for shaping and tack in place. Cut V-shape into each end of white ribbon; tie into a bow around Hat.

Feather (make 6)
Note: Make two sides each burgundy, gold, green lavender, purple and tan.

For **each side,** with color, ch 16, hdc in 2nd ch from hook, hdc in next 7 chs, dc in each of next 3 chs, tr in each of next 3 chs, 6 tr in last ch; working on opposite side of ch, tr in each of next 3 chs, dc in each of next 3 chs, hdc in last 8 chs, join with sl st in first hdc. Leaving 18" for sewing, fasten off.

Matching colors, sew two sides together. Sew Feathers to back of Body in fan shape. •

Country Bunnies
Continued from page 65

Rnd 4-7: Sc in each st around.

Rnd 8: (Sc in next st, sc next 2 sts tog) around (12). Stuff.

Rnd 9: (Sc in next st, sc next 2 sts tog) around (8).

Rnd 10: (Sc in each of next 2 sts, sc next 2 sts tog) around (6).

Rnds 11-12: Repeat rnds 2 and 3 of Victorian Bunny's Head & Body (12, 18).

Rnd 13: (Sc in next 8 sts, 2 sc in next st) around (20).

Rnds 14-16: Repeat rnd 4.

Rnd 17: (Sc in next 8 sts, sc next 2 sts tog) around (18).

Rnd 18: (Sc in next st, sc next 2 sts tog) around (12). Stuff.

Rnd 19: (Sc next 2 sts tog) around, join with sl st in first sc. Leaving 8" for sewing, fasten off (6).

Sew opening closed.

Arm (make 2)
Rnd 1: With off-white, ch 2, 6 sc in 2nd ch from hook (6 sc).

Rnds 2-6: Sc in each st around. At end of last rnd, join with sl st in first sc. Leaving 8" for sewing, fasten off.

Stuff. Flatten last rnd and sew Arms over rnd 11 on each side of Body.

Leg (make 2)
Rnd 1: With off-white, ch 2, 8 sc in 2nd ch from hook (8 sc).

Rnds 2-10: Sc in each st around. At end of last rnd, join with sl st in first sc. Leaving 8" for sewing, fasten off.

Stuff. Flatten last rnd and sew Legs to bottom of Body.

Ear (make 2)
Rnd 1: With off-white, ch 2, 6 sc in 2nd ch from hook (6 sc).

Rnd 2: (Sc in next st, 2 sc in next st) around (9).

Rnds 3-16: Sc in each st around. At end of last rnd, join with sl st in first sc. Leaving 8" for sewing, fasten off.

Flatten last rnd and fold in half, sew Ears to top of Head over rnd 1.

With slate blue, using French Knot (see page 159), embroider eyes over rnd 4 of Head ½" apart.

With pink, using Satin Stitch (see page 159), embroider nose over rnd 6 centered below eyes.

Cut ¼" wide piece off one long side of 12" piece gingham ribbon, tie in bow around Bunny's neck. With pinking shears, cut red fabric into oval shape, place in basket. Place Bunny in basket. If desired, glue red fabric and Bunny in place to secure. •

Christmas Elves

Designed by Alma Shields

Finished Size

Each Elf is 13" tall.

Materials For All Three

- ○ Worsted-weight yarn — 3 oz. each peach, green and dk. red, 2 oz. navy, 1 oz. each black, bright red, brown, gray, off white, tan and white
- ○ Size 5 pearl cotton — small amount each black, red and white
- ○ Powder blush
- ○ 2 stitch markers or bobby pins
- ○ Polyester fiberfill
- ○ Tapestry needle
- ○ No. 6 steel and H crochet hooks or sizes needed to obtain gauges

Gauges

With **No. 6 steel crochet hook and size-5 pearl cotton,** Eye = ⅝" x ⅞". With **H hook and worsted-weight yarn,** 7 sc = 2"; 7 sc rows = 2".

Notes: Do not join rnds unless otherwise stated. Mark first st of each rnd.

Use F hook and worsted-weight yarn unless otherwise stated.

See Individual Elf for specific colors.

Basic Elf
Head & Body

Rnd 1: Starting at **top of Head,** with peach, ch 2, 6 sc in 2nd ch from hook (6 sc).

Rnd 2: 2 sc in each st around (12).

Rnd 3: (Sc in next st, 2 sc in next st) around (18).

Rnd 4: (Sc in each of next 2 sts, 2 sc in next st) around (24).

Rnd 5: (Sc in each of next 3 sts, 2 sc in next st) around (30).

Rnds 6-8: Sc in each st around.

Rnd 9: Sc in first 5 sts, 2 sc in each of next 5 sts; for **center front of Head,** sc in next 10 sts; 2 sc in each of next 5 sts, sc in last 5 sts (40).

Rnds 10-14: Sc in each st around.

Rnd 15: Sc in first 8 sts, (sc next 2 sts tog) 5 times, sc in next 10 sts, (sc next 2 sts tog) 5 times, sc in each of last 2 sts (30).

Rnd 16: Sc in each st around.

Rnd 17: (Sc in each of next 3 sts, sc next 2 sts tog) around (24).

Rnd 18: (Sc in next 6 sts, sc next 2 sts tog) around (21).

Rnd 19: (Sc in next 5 sts, sc next 2 sts tog) around (18).

Rnd 20: (Sc in next 4 sts, sc next 2 sts tog) around (15).

Rnd 21: Sc in each st around, join with sl st in first sc, fasten off. Stuff.

Rnd 22: Join shirt color with sc in st at center back, sc in each st around.

Rnd 23: Working this rnd in **back lps** only, 2 sc in each st around.

Rnds 24-25: Sc in each st around.

Rnd 26: (Sc in next 9 sts, 2 sc in next st) around (33).

Rnd 27: Sc in each st around.

Rnd 28: (Sc in next 10 sts, 2 sc in next st) around (36).

Rnds 29-30: Sc in each st around.

Rnd 31: Working this rnd in **back lps** only, sc in each st around.

Rnds 32-33: Sc in each st around.

Rnd 34: (Sc in next 4 sts, sc next 2 sts tog) around (30).

Rnd 35: (Sc in each of next 3 sts, sc next 2 sts tog) around (24).

Rnd 36: (Sc in each of next 2 sts, sc next 2 sts tog) around (18).

Rnd 37: (Sc next st, sc next 2 sts tog) around (12).

Rnd 38: (Sc next 2 sts tog) around, join with sl st in first sc, fasten off (6). Stuff. Sew opening closed.

Collar

Working in **front lps** of rnd 22; mark first 2 sts at center front, holding botxtom of Body towards you, join shirt color with sl st in st at center back, ch 3, dc in each st around to one st before marked sts, (2 dc, hdc) in next st, sl st in each of next 2 marked sts, (hdc, 2 dc) in next st, dc in each st around, join with sl st in top of ch-3, fasten off.

For **lower edge of shirt,** working in **front lps** of rnd 30, holding Head towards you, working same as Collar.

Sleeve (make 2)

Rnd 1: With shirt color, ch 10, sl st in first ch to form ring, ch 1, sc in each ch around, join with sl st in first sc (10 sc).

Rnd 2: Ch 1, sc in each st around, join.

Rnd 3: Ch 1, 2 sc in first st, sc in each st around, join (11).

Rnds 4-12: Repeat rnds 2 and 3 alternately, ending with rnd 2 and 15 sts in last rnd. At end of last rnd, fasten off.

Continued on page 84

Christmas Elves

Continued from page 83

Hand

Rnd 1: With peach, leaving 6" end, ch 9, sl st in first ch to form ring, ch 1, sc in each ch around, join with sl st in first sc (9 sc).

Rnd 2: Ch 1, sc in each st around, join

Rnd 3: Ch 1, sc in first st; for **thumb,** ch 3, sl st in 2nd ch from hook, sc in next ch; sc in each st around, join.

Row 4: Working in rows, ch 1, sc in first st, skip sts on thumb; flatten last rnd; working through both thicknesses, sc in each st across, turn (5 sc).

Row 5: Ch 1, sc in first st; for **fingers,** (ch 3, sl st in 2nd ch from hook, sl st in next ch, sl st in next st on last row) 2 times, (ch 4, sl st in 2nd ch from hook, sl st in each of next 2 chs, sl st in next st on last row) 2 times, fasten off.

Weave 6" end on rnd 1 through starting chs; pull to gather slightly, secure. With thumb pointing up, insert Hand inside last rnd of Sleeve as shown in photo. Flatten Sleeve and sew Hand to Sleeve, sew remainder of Sleeve opening closed. Stuff Sleeve lightly.

Flatten rnd 1 of each Sleeve and sew at an angle over rnds 24-27 on each side of Body.

Leg (make 2)

Rnd 1: For **shoe,** with black, ch 2, 3 sc in 2nd ch from hook (3 sc).

Rnd 2: Sc in each st around.

Rnd 3: 2 sc in first st, 2 hdc in next st, 2 sc in last st (6 sts).

Rnd 4: Sc in each of first 2 sts, hdc in each of next 3 sts, sc in last st.

Rnd 5: Sc in first st, 2 sc in next st, hdc in next st, hdc in next st, 2 hdc in next st, hdc in next st, 2 sc in last st (9).

Rnd 6: Sc in each of first 2 sts; for **ankle opening,** ch 15;

sc in last 7 sts (15 chs, 9 sc).

Rnd 7: Sc in each st and in each ch around (24 sc).

Rnd 8: Sc in each st around.

Rnd 9: (Sc in next 4 sts, sc next 2 sts tog) around (20).

Rnd 10: (Sc next 2 sts tog) around, join with sl st in first sc, fasten off (10 sc). Sew sts tog on last rnd. Stuff.

Rnd 11: For **stocking,** working on opposite side of chs on ankle opening, join first color with sc in ch at center back, sc in next 5 chs, skip next 3 chs, sc in last 6 chs, join (12 sc).

Rnd 12: Ch 1, sc in each st around, join, fasten off.

Rnd 13: Join second color with sc in first st, sc in each st around, join, fasten off.

Rnd 14: Join first color with sc in first st, sc in each st around, join.

Rnds 15-27: Repeat rnds 12-14 consecutively, ending with rnd 12. Stuff. Flatten last rnd and sew opening closed. With black, sew 3 skipped chs on ankle opening together.

Sew Legs to bottom of Body.

Pants

Rnd 1: With Pants color, ch 36, sl st in first ch to form ring, ch 1, sc in each ch around, join with sl st in first sc (36 sc).

Rnds 2-7: Ch 1, sc in each st around, join.

Rnd 8: For **first leg,** ch 1, sc in first 18 sts leaving remaining sts unworked, ch 3, join with sl st in first sc (18 sc, 3 chs).

Rnd 9: Ch 1, sc in each st and in each ch around, join (21 sc).

Rnds 10-11: Ch 1, sc in each st around, join. At end of last rnd, fasten off.

Rnd 8: For **second leg,** join Pants color with sc in first skipped st on rnd 7, sc in each st around; working on opposite side of ch-3 on first leg, sl st in each of last 3 chs, join (21 sts).

Rnd 9-11: Ch 1, sc in each st

around, join. At end of last rnd, fasten off.

Place Pants on Elf; sew rnd 1 of Pants to rnd 31 of Elf's Body under lower edge of shirt.

Ear (make 2)

Row 1: With peach, ch 2, 3 sc in 2nd ch from hook, turn (3 sc).

Row 2: Ch 1, 2 sc in each st across, turn (6).

Row 3: Ch 1, sc in first st, (hdc, ch 2, sl st in 2nd ch from hook, hdc) in next st, hdc in next st, sc in each of last 3 sts, fasten off.

Sew Ears over rnds 10-14 on each side of Head.

Nose

Rnd 1: With peach, ch 2, 6 sc in 2nd ch from hook (6 sc).

Rnd 2: (2 sc in next st, sc in next st) around (9).

Rnd 3: Sc in each st around, join with sl st in first sc, fasten off.

Sew Nose over rnds 11-13 on center front of Head.

Eye (make 2)

With No. 6 steel hook and white pearl cotton, ch 5, 4 hdc in 3rd ch from hook, hdc in next ch, 5 hdc in last ch; working on opposite side of ch, hdc in next ch, join with sl st in top of ch-2, fasten off (12 hdc).

For **pupil** (make 2), with No. 6 steel hook and black pearl cotton, ch 3, 11 hdc in 3rd ch from hook, join with sl st in top of ch-2, fasten off.

Sew Eyes ½" apart over rnds 8-10 centered above Nose.

Sew one pupil over bottom half of one Eye with bottom of pupil overlapping bottom edge of Eye.

Repeat on other Eye.

Facial Features

1: For **Eye indentations,** insert tapestry needle threaded with peach through back of Head to bottom of Eye, make small stitch; inset needle back through Head to bottom of next Eye, make small stitch, push needle back through Head to center back, pull to indent; secure ends.

2: For **mouth,** with No. 6 steel hook and red pearl cotton, ch 10, fasten off. Sew to rnd 14 centered below Nose as shown in photo.

3: With red pearl cotton, embroider one Straight Stitch (see page 159) on each end of mouth.

4: Brush cheeks with blush.

Hat

Rnd 1: With Hat color, ch 2, 6 sc in 2nd ch from hook (6 sc).

Rnd 2: Sc in each st around.

Rnd 3: (Sc in next st, 2 sc in next st) around (9).

Rnd 4: (Sc in each of next 2 sts, 2 sc in next st) around (12).

Rnd 5: (Sc in each of next 3 sts, 2 sc in next st) around (15).

Rnd 6: (Sc in next 4 sts, 2 sc in next st) around (18).

Rnd 7: (Sc in next 5 sts, 2 sc in next st) around (21).

Rnd 8: (Sc in next 6 sts, 2 sc in next st) around (24).

Rnd 9: (Sc in next 7 sts, 2 sc in next st) around (27).

Rnd 10: (Sc in next 8 sts, 2 dc in next st) around (30).

Rnds 11-12: Repeat rnds 4 and 5 (40, 50). At end of last rnd, join with sl st in first sc.

Rnd 13: Ch 1; working from left to right, **reverse sc** (see page 159), in each st around, join, fasten off.

ELF NO. 1

Work basic Elf beginning on page 83 using dk. red for shirt color, bright red for first stocking color, white for sec-ond stocking color and green for Pants and Hat color.

Apron

Row 1: With off-white, ch 15, sc in 2nd ch from hook, sc in each ch across, turn (14 sc).

Rows 2-4: Ch 1, sc in each st across, turn.

Row 5: Ch 1, sc first 2 sts tog, sc in each st across to last 2 sts, sc last 2 sts tog, turn (12).

Rows 6-7: Repeat row 2.

Rows 8-16: Repeat rows 5-7 consecutively, ending with 6 sts in last row. At end of last row, fasten off.

Row 17: Join off-white with sc in end of row 1, sc in end of each row across; for **neck loop,** ch 16; working on opposite side of Apron, sc in end of row 16, sc in end of each row across, fasten off.

For **tie (make 2),** with off-white, ch 30, fasten off. Sew one tie to each end of row 10. Place neck loop over Elf's Head; tie Apron around waist.

Finishing

1: For **hair,** with tapestry needle and 2 strands of gray, using Satin Stitch (see page 159), embroider strands in varying lengths around Head from rnd 6 in front to rnd 15 in back as shown in photo.

2: Using uniform Satin Stitches embroider **beard** around lower edge of face from Ear to Ear as shown.

3: Sew Hat to Head covering upper ends of hair strands.

ELF NO. 2

Work Basic Elf beginning on page 83 using green for shirt color, navy for first stocking color, white for second stocking color and dk. red for Pants and Hat color.

Finishing

1: For **belt,** cut one strand of tan 4 yds. long, fold in half, place fold around doorknob. Holding ends together, twist yarn tightly in one direction. Still holding same ends, fold in half again and let yarn twist around itself naturally. Cut loop from doorknob. Tie knot 1" from each end. Clip loops and trim ends. Tie belt in knot around Elf's waist.

2: For **beard,** with brown, ch 20, fasten off. Cut 40 strands brown each 4" long. For each fringe, holding 2 strands together, fold in half, insert hook in ch, draw fold through, draw all loose ends through fold, tighten. Fringe in each ch across ch-20. Brush fringe and trim ends as desired. Sew around lower edge of face from Ear to Ear as shown in photo.

3: For **hair,** with 2 strand brown, work same as Elf No.1's hair.

4: Sew Hat to Head covering upper ends of hair strands.

ELF NO. 3

Work Basic Elf beginning on page 83 using navy for shirt and Hat color, white for first stocking color, dk. red for second stocking color and green for Pants color.

Finishing

1: For **belt,** using brown, work same as Elf No. 2's belt.

2: For **hair,** with 2 strands tan, work sam as Elf No. 1's hair.

3: Sew Hat to Head covering upper ends of hair strands. •

Finished Size

Witch is 5" tall.

Materials

○ Size 10 bedspread cotton —
90 yds. black, and 25
yds violet;
○ 30" orange ⅛" satin ribbon
○ 4¼" fashion doll with long
black hair
○ 2 straight pins
○ Tapestry needle
○ No. 3 steel crochet hook or
size needed to obtain gauge

Gauge

7 sc = 1"; 8 sc rows = 1".

Littlest Witch

Designed by Beverly Mewhorter

Dress
Bodice
Row 1: Starting at **waist,** with black, ch 19, sc in 2nd ch from hook, sc in each ch across, turn (18 sc).

Row 2: Ch 1, sc in first 4 sts; (for **armhole,** ch 6, skip next 3 sts; sc in next 4 sts) 2 times, turn (12 sc, 2 ch-6 sps).

Row 3: Ch 1, sc in each st and in each ch across, turn (24 sc).

Row 4: Ch 1, sc in each of first 2 sts, sc next 2 sts tog, (sc in next 2 sts, sc next 2 sts tog) across, turn (18).

Row 5: Ch 1, sc in each of first 2 sts, (sc next 2 sts tog) 7 times, sc in each of last 2 sts, fasten off (11).

Sleeves
Rnd 1: Working around one armhole, join black with sc in 2nd skipped st at underarm, sc in next st, 2 sc in each of next 6 chs, sc in last st, join with sl st in first sc (15 sc).

Rnds 2-7: Ch 1, sc in each st around, join.

Rnd 8: Ch 1, sc in each of first 2 sts, (sc next 2 sts tog) 6 times, sc in last st, join (9).

Rnd 9: Ch 1, 2 sc in each st around, join, fasten off (18).
Repeat on other armhole.

Skirt
Row 1: Working in starting ch on opposite side of row 1 on Bodice, with right side facing you, join black with sc in first ch, 2 sc in same ch, 3 sc in each ch across, turn (54 sc).

Rows 2-17: Ch 1, sc in each st across, turn. At end of last row, fasten off.
Place Dress on doll. Sew back opening closed.
Cut 2 pieces of ribbon each 8" long. Tie one piece into a bow around rnd 8 on each Sleeve. Tie remaining ribbon into a bow around waist.

Cape
Row 1: With violet, ch 11, sc in 2nd ch from hook, sc in each ch across, turn (10 sc).

Row 2: Ch 1, 2 sc in each st across, turn (20).

Row 3: Ch 1, sc in first st, (ch 6, sc in next st) across, turn (20 sc, 19 ch-6 sps).

Rows 4-5: Ch 6, sc in first ch sp, (ch 6, sc in next ch sp) across, turn. At end of last row, fasten off.

Row 6: Working in starting ch on opposite side of row 1, with right side of facing you, join violet with sc in first ch, 2 sc in same ch, 3 sc in each ch across, fasten off.
Sew row 1 of Cape to back of shoulders on Dress.

Hat
Crown
Rnd 1: With black, ch 30, sl st in first ch to form ring, ch 1, sc in each ch around, join with sl st in first sc (30 sc).

Rnd 2: Ch 1, sc in each st around, join.

Rnd 3: Ch 1, sc in each of first 2 sts, (sc next 2 sts tog, sc in each of next 2 sts) around, join (23).

Rnd 4: Repeat rnd 2.

Rnd 5: Ch 1, sc in each of first 3 sts, (sc next 2 sts tog, sc in each of next 2 sts) around, join (18).

Rnd 6: Repeat rnd 2.

Rnd 7: Ch 1, sc first 2 sts tog, (sc next 2 sts tog) around, join (9).

Rnds 8-10: Repeat rnd 2.

Rnd 11: Ch 1, sc in first st, (sc next 2 sts tog) around, join. Leaving 8" end for sewing, fasten off.
Sew opening on last rnd closed.

Brim
Rnd 1: Working in starting ch on opposite side of rnd 1 on Crown, with right side facing you, join black with sc in first ch, sc in same ch, 2 sc in each ch around, join with sl st in first sc (60 sc).

Rnd 2: Ch 1, sc in each of first 2 sts, 2 sc in next st, (sc in each of next 2 sts, 2 sc in next st) around, join (80).

Rnd 3: Ch 1, sc in each st around, join, fasten off.
Pin Hat to top of head. •

Chapter Four

Holidays in a Hurry

One moment you look at the
calendar and it's just an ordinary
day filled with the regular routine.
The next time you check, you
are two weeks shy of a holiday.
Where did the time go? There's
just enough time to crochet
up the perfect accent for
last-minute decorating.

Raffia Cozy

Designed by Carol Smith

Finished Size

Covers pot 8½" across top.

Materials

○ Raffia straw — 288 yds.
tan (A), 24 yds. each bright
pink (B) and lt. yellow (C),
12 yds. lt. green (D) and
6 yds. baby pink (E)
○ Tapestry needle
○ G crochet hook or size
needed to obtain gauge

Gauge

4 hdc = 1"; 4 hdc rows = 1¾".

Large Motif

Rnd 1: With C, ch 4, sl st in first
ch to form ring, ch 2, 15 hdc
in ring, join with sl st in top of
ch-2, fasten off (16).

Rnd 2: Working this rnd in
back lps, join B with sc in
any st, sc in each st around,
join, fasten off.

Rnd 3: Join E with sl st in any st,
(ch 2, dc, tr) in same st, (tr,
dc, hdc) in next st, sc in each
of next 2 sts, *(hdc, dc, tr) in
next st, (tr, dc, hdc) in next st,
sc in each of next 2 sts;
repeat from * around, join,
fasten off (32).

Rnd 4: Join B with sc in first st,
sc in same st, sc in next st, 2
sc in each of next 2 sts, sc in
next st, 2 sc in next st; working over next 2 sts on rnd 3
into sts on rnd 2, sc next 2 sts
on rnd 2 tog, (2 sc in next st,
sc in next st, 2 sc in each of

next 2 sts, sc in next st, 2 sc
in next st; working over next 2
sts on rnd 3 into sts on rnd 2,
sc next 2 sts on rnd 2 tog)
around, join with sl st in first
sc, fasten off (44 sts).

Rnd 5: Join D with sc in first st,
sc in next 3 sts, 2 sc in each
of next 2 sts, (sc in next 9 sts,
2 sc in each of next 2 sts) 3
times, sc in last 5 sts, join,
fasten off.

Small Motif (make 5)

Row 1: With A, ch 3, sl st in
first ch to form ring, ch 2, (2
hdc, ch 1, 3 hdc) in ring, turn
(6 hdc, 1 ch sp).

Rows 2-4: Ch 2, hdc in same st,
hdc in each st across with 2
hdc in last st and (2 hdc, ch 1,
2 hdc) in ch-1 sp, ending with
24 hdc and 1 ch sp on last
row. At end of last row, leaving
12" for sewing, fasten off.

Sew Small Motifs to Large Motifs
according to Assembly Diagram.

Top

Note: To **hdc next 4 sts tog,**
(yo, insert hook in next st,
yo draw lp through) 4 times,
yo, draw through all 9 lps
on hook.

Rnd 1: Working around outer
edge of Large Motifs, join A
with sl st as indicated on
diagram, ch 2, hdc in
same st, hdc in next
10 sts, hdc next 4 sts
tog, hdc in next 10 sts,
2 hdc in next st, ch 2, (2
hdc in next st, hdc in next
10 sts, hdc next 4 sts tog,

hdc in next 10 sts, 2 hdc in
next st, ch 2) around, join
with sl st in top of ch-2.

Note: For **decrease (dec);**
working in 2 sts before next
decrease, (yo, insert hook in
next st, yo, draw lp through) 2
times, skip next dec, (yo, insert
hook in next st, yo, draw lp
through) 2 times, yo, draw
through all 9 lps on hook.

Rnds 2-7: Ch 2, hdc in each st
around with **dec** at each
indentation and (2 hdc, ch 1,
2 hdc) in each ch sp. At end
of last rnd, fasten off.

Edging

Rnd 1: Working around bottom
edge of plant cozy, join A
with sl st in end of any row,
ch 2, hdc in end of each row
around, join with sl st in top
of ch-2.

Rnds 2-3: Ch 2, hdc in each st
around, join. At end of last
rnd, fasten off. •

ASSEMBLY DIAGRAM

Start Here
○ = Stitch
Large Motif
Large Motif
Small Motif

Sparkling Table Accents

Designed by Rosanne Kropp

Finished Size

Coaster is 4½" across.
Napkin Ring is 1½" wide.

Materials For One Set

○ Size 10 metallic bedspread cotton — 80 yds. each gold and white
○ Tapestry needle
○ No. 7 steel crochet hook or size needed to obtain gauge

Gauge

Rnds 1-3 of Coaster = 2½" across at widest point.

White Coaster

Rnd 1: With white, ch 5, sl st in first ch to form ring, ch 6, (sc in ring, ch 5) 5 times, join with sl st in first ch of ch-6 (6 ch lps).

Rnd 2: Sl st in first ch lp, ch 4, (2 tr, ch 3, 3 tr) in same lp, ch 1, *(3 tr, ch 3, 3 tr) in next ch lp, ch 1; repeat from * around, join with sl st in top of ch-4 (6 ch-3 sps, 6 ch-1 sps).

Rnd 3: Sl st in next 2 tr, sl st in next ch-3 sp, ch 3, (2 tr, ch 3, 2 tr, dc) in same sp, ch 1, (dc, ch 1, dc) in next ch-1 sp, ch 1, *(dc, 2 tr, ch 3, 2 tr, dc) in next ch-3 sp, ch 1, (dc, ch 1, dc) in next ch-1 sp, ch 1; repeat from * around, join with sl st in top of ch-3, fasten off.

Rnd 4: Join gold with sl st in first st, ch 3, *[dc in each of next 2 tr, (3 dc, ch 2, 3 dc) in next ch-3 sp, dc in each of next 2 tr, dc in next dc, dc in next ch-1 sp, dc in next dc, skip next ch-1 sp, dc in next dc, dc in next ch-1 sp], dc in next dc; repeat from * 4 more times; repeat between [ ], join, fasten off (96 dc, 6 ch-2 sps).

Rnd 5: Join white with sc in first st, sc in next 5 sts, *[ch 4, skip next ch-2 sp, sc in next 7 sts, ch 4, skip next 2 sts], sc in next 7 sts; repeat from * 4 more times; repeat between [ ], sc in last st, join with sl st in first sc (84 sc, 12 ch-4 sps).

Note: For **cluster (cl)**, *yo 2 times, insert hook in sp, yo, draw lp through, (yo, draw through 2 lps on hook) 2 times; repeat from * one more time in same sp, yo, draw through all 3 lps on hook.

Rnd 6: Sl st in next 2 sts, ch 1, skip next 3 sts, cl in next ch-4 sp, (ch 3, cl in same sp) 4 times, ch 1, skip next 3 sts, *sl st in next st, ch 1, skip next 3 sts, cl in next ch-4 sp, (ch 3, sl in same sp) 4 times, ch 1, skip next 3 sts, repeat from * around, join with sl st in 2nd sl st, fasten off.

Gold Coaster

Rnds 1-2: Repeat same rnds of White Coaster. At end of last rnd, fasten off.

Rnd 3: Join gold with sl st in any ch-3 sp, ch 3, (2 tr, ch 3, 2 tr, dc) in same sp, ch 1, (dc, ch 1, dc) in next ch-1 sp, ch 1, *(dc, 2 tr, ch 3, 2 tr, dc) in next ch-3 sp, ch 1, (dc, ch 1, dc) in next ch-1 sp, ch 1; repeat from * around, join with sl st in top of ch-3, fasten off.

Rnd 4: With white, repeat same rnd of White Coaster.

Rnds 5-6: With gold, repeat same rnds of White Coaster.

Napkin Ring (make 2 each gold and white)

Rnd 1: (Ch 6, cl in 6th ch from hook) 12 times, join with sl st in bottom of first cl (12 cls).

Rnd 2: Working around long edge, ch 5, (sl st in next sp between cls, ch 5) around, join with sl st in bottom of first ch-5 (12 ch-5 sps).

Note: For **picot,** ch 3, sl st in top of last sc made.

Rnd 3: For **first side,** sl st in first ch-5 sp, ch 4, (2 tr, ch 3, 3 tr) in same sp, (sc, picot) in next ch sp, *(3 tr, ch 3, 3 tr) in next ch sp, (sc, picot) in next ch sp; repeat from * around, join with sl st in top of ch-4, fasten off.

For **second side,** working on opposite side of ring, join with sl st in first ch sp, work same as first side. •

Floral Lid Covers

Designed by Patricia Hall

PINK COVER

Finished Size

Cover Fits over 3½" lid.

Materials

- ○ Worsted-weight yarn — small amount lt. pink
- ○ Size 10 bedspread cotton — small amount each green, dk. pink and yellow
- ○ 24" lt. pink ⅝" satin ribbon
- ○ Tapestry needle
- ○ No. 7 steel, G and H crochet hooks or sizes needed to obtain gauges

Gauges

With **No. 7 hook and bedspread cotton,** rnd 1 of Flower = ¾" across. With **H hook and worsted-weight,** rnds 1-3 of Cover = 3½" across.

Cover

Rnd 1: With H hook and lt. pink worsted-weight, ch 3, sl st in first ch to form ring, ch 3, 11 dc in ring, join with sl st in top of ch-3 (12 dc).

Rnds 2-3: Ch 3, dc in same st, 2 dc in each st around, join (24, 48). Change to G hook.

Rnd 4: Working this rnd in **back lps** only, ch 4, skip next st, (sc in next st, ch 1, skip next st) around, join with sl st in 3rd ch of ch-4 (24 ch sps).

Rnd 5: Ch 1, sc in each dc and in each ch sp around, join with sl st in first sc (48).

Notes: For **beginning shell (beg shell),** ch 3, (dc, ch 2, 2 dc) in same st or sp.

For **shell,** (2 dc, ch 2, 2 dc) in next st or ch sp.

Rnd 6: Beg shell, skip next 3 sts, (shell in next st, skip next 3 sts) around, join with sl st in top of ch-3 (12 shells).

Rnd 7: Sl st in next st, sl st in next ch sp, beg shell, shell in ch sp of each shell around, join, fasten off.

For **trim,** with No. 7 hook and dk. pink bedspread cotton, join with sc in any sp between shells, ch 4, (2 sc, 2 dc, 2 sc) in next ch sp, ch 4, *sc in next sp between shells, ch 4, (2 sc, 2 dc, 2 sc) in next ch sp, ch 4; repeat from * around, join with sl st in first sc, fasten off.

Flower

Rnd 1: With No. 7 hook and dk. pink bedspread cotton, ch 6, sl st in first ch to form ring, ch 3, 23 dc in ring, join with sl st in top of ch-3 (24 dc).

Rnd 2: Ch 4, skip next 3 sts, (sl st in next st, ch 4, skip next 3 sts) around, join with sl st in joining sl st of last rnd (6 ch sps).

Rnd 3: Sl st in next ch sp, ch 1, (sc, hdc, dc, 3 tr, dc, hdc, sc) in same sp and in each ch sp around, join with sl st in first sc, fasten off (6 petals).

Rnd 4: Working behind petals, with No. 7 hook and dk. pink bedspread cotton, join with sl st in 3rd st of any skipped 3-dc group on rnd 1, ch 4, (sl st in 3rd st of next skipped 3-dc group on rnd 1, ch 4) around, join with sl st in first sl st (6 ch sps).

Note: For **double treble crochet (dtr),** yo 3 times, insert hook in next st, yo, draw lp through, (yo, draw through 2 lps on hook) 4 times.

Rnd 5: Sl st in next ch sp, ch 1, (sc, ch 2, tr, 5 dtr, tr, ch 2, sc) in same sp and in each ch sp around, join with sl st in first sc, fasten off (6 petals).

Rnd 6: Join green with sc in center dtr of any petal on rnd 5, ch 5, dc in first sc of next petal, ch 5, (sc in center dtr of next petal, ch 5, dc in first sc of next petal, ch 5) around, join (6 dc, 6 sc).

Rnd 7: Ch 1, (sc, ch 6, sc) in same st, ch 5, (sc, ch 7, sc) in next dc, ch 5, *(sc, ch 6, sc) in next sc, ch 5, (sc, ch 7, sc) in next dc, ch 5; repeat from * around, join with sl st in first sc, fasten off.

For **center,** with No. 7 hook and yellow bedspread cotton, ch 3, 2 dc in 3rd ch from hook, sl st in same ch, fasten off.

Tack to center of rnd 1. Sew ch-6 and ch-7 lps of rnd 7 on Flower to every 4th st of rnd 3 on Cover. Weave ribbon through ch sps of rnd 4 on Cover. Tie ends into a bow.

BLUE COVER

Finished Size

Cover Fits over 3½" lid.

Continued on page 96

Floral Lid Covers
Continued from page 95

Materials

○ Worsted-weight yarn — small amount lt. blue; size 10 bedspread cotton — small amount each royal blue, green and yellow
○ 24" royal blue ⅝" satin ribbon
○ Tapestry needle
○ No. 7 steel, G and H crochet hooks or sizes needed to obtain gauges

Gauges

With **No. 7 hook and bedspread cotton,** Small Section of Flower = 2" across. With **H hook and worsted-weight,** rnds 1-3 of Cover = 3½" across.

Cover
Rnds 1-5: With lt. blue worsted-weight, repeat same rnds of Pink Cover, ending with 48 sc.
Rnd 6: Ch 1, (sc in next st, ch 5, skip next 3 sts) around, join (12 sc, 12 ch sps).
Rnd 7: Ch 8, (dc in next sc, ch 5) around, join with sl st in 3rd ch of ch-8.
Rnd 8: Ch 6; working over ch-5 sp on last rnd, sc in next ch-5 sp on rnd 6, ch 3, *dc in next dc; working over ch-5 sp on last rnd, sc in ch-5 sp on rnd 6, ch 3; repeat from * around, join with sl st in 3rd ch of ch-6, fasten off (24 ch-3 sps, 12 dc, 12 sc).
For **trim,** with No. 7 hook and royal blue bedspread cotton, join with sc in any sc, ch 6, sc in next dc, (ch 6, sc) 3 times in same dc, ch 6, *sc in next sc, ch 6, sc in next dc, (ch 6, sc) 3 times in same dc, ch 6; repeat from * around, join with sl st in first sc, fasten off.

Leaves
Rnd 1: With No. 7 hook and green bedspread cotton, ch 6, sl st in first ch to form ring, ch 3, 23 dc in ring, join with sl st in top of ch-3 (24 dc).
Note: For **picot,** ch 3, sl st in top of last st made.
Rnd 2: Ch 10, (3 tr, picot, 2 tr, ch 3, sl st) in 4th ch from hook, ch 6, skip next 2 sts, *sl st in next st, ch 10, (3 tr, picot, 2 tr, ch 3, sl st) in 4th ch from hook, ch 6, skip next 2 sts; repeat from * around, join with sl st in joining sl st of last rnd, fasten off (8 Leaves).
Tack to rnds 1-3 of Cover.

Flower
Large Section
Rnd 1: With No. 7 steel hook and royal blue bedspread cotton, ch 6, sl st in first ch to form ring, ch 3, 13 dc in ring, join with sl st in top of ch-3 (14 dc).
Rnd 2: Ch 8, sc in 2nd ch from hook, sc in next ch, hdc in next 4 chs, sc in last ch, (sl st in next st, ch 8, sc in 2nd ch from hook, sc in next ch, hdc in next 4 chs, sc in last ch) around, join with sl st in joining sl st of last rnd, fasten off (14 petals).

Small Section
Rnd 1: With No. 7 steel hook and royal blue bedspread cotton, ch 6, sl st in first ch to form ring, ch 3, 7 dc in ring, join with sl st in top of ch-3 (8 dc).
Rnd 2: Repeat same rnd of Large Section (8 petals).
Holding Small Section on top of Large Section, tack together through middle.
For **center,** with No. 7 hook and yellow bedspread cotton, ch 3, 2 dc in 3rd ch from hook, sl st in same ch, fasten off.
Tack to middle of Flower over

Small Section. Center and tack Flower over Leaves. Weave ribbon through ch sps of rnd 4 on Cover. Tie ends into a bow.

LAVENDER COVER

Finished Size

Cover Fits over 3½" lid.

Materials

○ Worsted-weight yarn — small amount lavender
○ Size 10 bedspread cotton — small amount each green, purple and yellow
○ 24" lavender ⅝" satin ribbon
○ Tapestry needle
○ No. 7 steel, G and H crochet hooks or sizes needed to obtain gauges

Gauges

With **No. 7 hook and bedspread cotton,** Flower = 1¼" across. With **H hook and worsted-weight,** rnds 1-3 of Cover = 3½" across.

Cover
Rnds 1-5: With lavender, repeat same rnds of Pink Cover, ending with 48 sc.
Rnd 6: Ch 1, sc in each st around, join.
Note: For **double treble crochet (dtr),** yo 3 times, insert hook in next st, yo, draw lp through, (yo, draw through 2 lps on hook) 4 times.
Rnd 7: Ch 1, (sc in next st, hdc in next st, dc in next st, tr in next st, 5 dtr in next st, tr in next st, dc in next st, hdc in next st) around, join, fasten off (72 sts).
For **trim,** with No. 7 hook and purple bedspread cotton, join with sc in any st, ch 3, (sc in

Continued on page 107

Jack-o'-Lantern Basket

Designed by Zelda Workman

Finished Size

Basket is 2" tall not including Handle.

Materials

○ Size 3 crochet cotton —
  25 yds. orange and small
  amount black
○ Tapestry needle
○ C crochet hook or size
  needed to obtain gauge

Gauge

6 sc = 1"; 6 sc rows = 1".

Jack-o'-Lantern

Note: Do not join rnds unless
  otherwise stated. Mark first st
  of each rnd.
Rnd 1: With orange, ch 4,
  15 dc in 4th ch from hook
  (16 dc).
Rnd 2: (Sc in next st, 2 sc in
  next st) around (24 sc).
Rnd 3: (2 sc in next st, sc
  in each of next 3 sts)
  around (30).
Rnd 4: (Sc in next 9 sts, 2 sc in
  next st) around (33).
Rnd 5: (Sc in next 10 sts, 2 sc in
  next st) around (36).
Rnds 6-10: Sc in each st around.
Rnd 11: (Sc in next 4 sts, sc next
  2 sts tog) around (30).
Rnd 12: (Sc in each of next 3 sts,
  sc next 2 sts tog) around (24).
Rnd 13: Sl st in each st around,
  join with sl st in first sl st,
  fasten off.

Handle

With black, ch 24, sl st in 2nd ch
  from hook, sl st in each ch
  across, fasten off.
Sew one end to each side of rnd
  12 on Jack-o'-Lantern.

Finishing

With black, using Straight Stitch
  (see page 159), embroider
  eyes, nose and **mouth** as
  shown in photo. •

Holidays in a Hurry

Finished Size

Coaster is 5¾" across.
Napkin Edging is ½" wide.

Materials For One of Each

❍ Size 10 bedspread cotton —
   300 yds. desired color
❍ 17" square cotton napkin
❍ No. 6 steel crochet hook or size
   needed to obtain gauge.

Gauge

Rnds 1-2 of Coaster = 1⅜" across.
Edging is ½" wide.

Falling Leaves

Designed by Judy Teague Treece

Coaster

Rnd 1: Ch 5, sl st in first ch to form ring, ch 3, 23 dc in ring, join with sl st in top of ch-3 (24 dc).

Rnd 2: Ch 3, dc in next st, ch 5, skip next 2 sts, (dc in each of next 2 sts, ch 5, skip next 2 sts) around, join (12 dc, 6 ch-5 sps).

Rnd 3: Ch 3, dc in same st, 2 dc in next st, ch 3, sc in next ch-5 sp, ch 3, (2 dc in each of next 2 sts, ch 3, sc in next ch-5 sp, ch 3) around, join (24 dc, 12 ch-3 sps).

Rnd 4: Ch 3, dc in same st, 2 dc in next st *[ch 2, 2 dc in each of next 2 sts, ch 3, (sc in next ch-3 sp, ch 3) 2 times], 2 dc in each of next 2 sts; repeat from * 4 more times; repeat between [ ], join (18 ch-3 sps, 6 ch-2 sps).

Notes: For **beginning cluster (beg cl),** ch 3, (yo, insert hook in same sp, yo, draw lp through, yo, draw through 2 lps on hook) 2 times, yo, draw through all 3 lps on hook.

For **cluster (cl),** yo, insert hook in next ch sp, yo, draw lp through, yo, draw through 2 lps on hook, (yo, insert hook in same sp, yo, draw lp through, yo, draw through 2 lps on hook) 2 times, yo, draw through all 4 lps on hook.

Rnd 5: Sl st in each of next 3 sts, sl st in next ch-2 sp, beg cl, (ch 2, cl in same sp) 2 times, *[ch 4, sc in next ch-3 sp, ch 3, cl in next ch-3 sp, ch 3, sc in next ch-3 sp, ch 4], (cl, ch 2, cl, ch 2, cl) in next ch-2 sp; repeat from * 4 more times; repeat between [ ], join with sl st in top of beg cl (12 ch-4 sps, 12 ch-3 sps, 12 ch-2 sps).

Rnd 6: Sl st in first ch-2 sp, ch 1, sc in same sp, *[ch 5, sc in next ch-2 sp, ch 4, skip next ch-4 sp, skip next ch-3 sp, (cl, ch 2, cl, ch 2, cl) in next cl, ch 4, skip next ch-3 sp, skip next ch-4 sp], sc in next ch-2 sp; repeat from * 4 more times; repeat between [ ], join with sl st in first sc (12 ch-4 sps, 12 ch-2 sps, 6 ch-5 sps).

Rnd 7: Sl st in first ch-5 sp, ch 3, 8 dc in same sp, *[ch 4, skip next ch-4 sp, (cl, ch 2, cl) in next ch-2 sp, ch 2, (cl, ch 2, cl) in next ch-2 sp, ch 4, skip next ch-4 sp], 9 dc in next ch-5 sp, repeat from * 4 more times; repeat between [ ], join with sl st in top of ch-3 (54 dc, 18 ch-2 sps, 12 ch-4 sps).

Rnd 8: Ch 4, dc in next dc, (ch 1, dc in next dc) 7 times, *[ch 4, skip next ch-4 sp, (cl, ch 2, cl) in next ch-2 sp, ch 2, skip next ch-2 sp, (cl, ch 2, cl) in next ch-2 sp, ch 4, skip next ch-4 sp], dc in next dc, (ch 1, dc in next dc) 8 times; repeat from * 4 more times; repeat between [ ], join wth sl st in 3rd ch of ch-4.

Rnd 9: Sl st in first ch-1 sp, ch 1, sc in same sp, *[(ch 2, sc in next ch-1 sp) 7 times, ch 3, skip next ch-4 sp, (cl, ch 2, cl) in next ch-2 sp, ch 2, skip next ch-2 sp, (cl, ch 2, cl) in next ch-2 sp, ch 3, skip next ch-4 sp], sc in next ch-1 sp; repeat from * 4 more times; repeat between [ ], join with sl st in first sc.

Rnd 10: Sl st in first ch-2 sp, ch 1, sc in same sp, *[(ch 2, sc in next ch-2 sp) 6 times, ch 3, skip next ch-3 sp, (cl, ch 2, cl) in next ch-2 sp, ch 2, skip next ch-2 sp, (cl, ch 2, cl) in next ch-2 sp, ch 3, skip next ch-3 sp], sc in next ch-2 sp; repeat from * 4 more times; repeat between [ ], join, fasten off.

Edging

Rnd 1: Place slip knot on hook; working around outer edge of napkin, push hook through fabric, yo, draw lp through, yo, draw through 2 lps on hook (first sc made), ch 1; spacing sts approximately 1/8" apart, (sc, ch 1) around, ending with an even number of sts, join with sl st in first sc.

Rnd 2: Sl st in first ch sp, ch 1, (sc, hdc, dc, tr, dc, hdc, sc) in same sp, sc in next ch sp, *(sc, hdc, dc, tr, dc, hdc, sc) in next ch sp, sc in next ch sp; repeat from * around, join, fasten off. •

Mistletoe Stocking

Designed by Katherine Eng

Finished Size

Stocking is 13½" long not including hanger.

Materials

- ○ Worsted-weight yarn — 3 oz. burgundy/green/beige variegated and 1 oz. burgundy
- ○ 32" burgundy ⅞" satin ribbon
- ○ Tapestry needle
- ○ G crochet hook or size needed to obtain gauge

Gauge

4 dc = 1"; one sc row and one dc row = 1".

Front

Row 1: With variegated, ch 40, sc in 2nd ch from hook, (ch 1, skip next ch, sc in next ch) across, turn (20 sc, 19 ch sps).

Row 2: Ch 3, dc in same st, dc in each ch sp and in each st across, turn (40 dc). Front of row 2 is right side of work.

Row 3: Ch 1, sc in first st, (ch 1, skip next st, sc in next st) across to last st, ch 1, sc in last st, turn (21 sc, 20 ch sps).

Row 4: Ch 3, dc in each ch sp and in each st across, turn (41 dc).

Row 5: Ch 1, sc in first st, (ch 1, skip next st, sc in next st) across, turn.

Rows 6-11: Repeat rows 2-5 consecutively, ending with row 3 and 23 sc and 22 ch sps.

Row 12: For **toe**, ch 3, dc in next ch sp, (dc in next st, dc in next ch sp) 6 times leaving remaining sts unworked, turn (14 dc).

Rnd 13: Ch 1, skip first st, sc in next st, (ch 1, skip next st, sc in next st) across, turn (7 sc, 6 ch sps).

Row 14: Repeat row 4 (13 dc).

Row 15: Ch 1, sc in first st, (ch 1, skip next st, sc in next st) across, turn.

Row 16: Ch 3, dc in next ch sp, (dc in next st, dc in next ch sp) across leaving last st unworked, turn (12 dc).

Row 17: Repeat row 13 (6 sc, 5 ch sps).

Row 18: Repeat row 16 (10 dc).

Row 19: Ch 1, skip first st, sc in next st, ch 1, skip next st, (sc in next st, ch 1, skip next st) 2 times, sc next 2 sts tog leaving last st unworked, fasten off.

Edging

Row 1: With right side facing you, working in starting ch on opposite side of row 1, join variegated with sl st in first ch, ch 3, dc in next 11 chs, hdc in next 12 chs, sc in each of next 3 chs; for **heel shaping,** hdc in each of next 3 chs, dc in next 4 chs, 2 dc in next ch, hdc in each of next 3 chs, 2 sc in last ch; working in ends of rows across bottom, sc in each sc row and 2 sc in each dc row across to row 19; for **toe shaping,** working in sts across row 19, 2 sc in first st, hdc in next ch sp, hdc in next st, 3 dc in next ch sp, hdc in next st, hdc in next ch sp, 2 sc in last st; working in ends of rows across top, 2 sc in each dc row and sc in each sc row across to row 12; working in unworked sts across row 11, 2 sc in first st, (sc in next ch sp, sc in next st) 4 times, (hdc in next ch sp, hdc in next st) 5 times, (dc in next ch sp, dc in next st) 6 times, **do not turn,** fasten off.

Row 2: Join burgundy with sc in first st, sc in each st across, fasten off.

Back

Rows 1-11: Repeat same rows of Stocking Front. At end of last row, fasten off.

Row 12: Join variegated with sl st in 16th ch sp, ch 3, dc in each st and in each ch sp across, turn (14 dc).

Row 13: Ch 1, sc in first st, (ch 1, skip next st, sc in next st) across leaving last st unworked, turn (7 sc, 6 ch sps).

Row 14: Ch 3, dc in each st and in each ch sp across, turn (13 dc).

Row 15: Ch 1, sc in first st, (ch 1, skip next st, sc in next st) across, turn (7 sc, 6 ch sps).

Row 16: Sl st in next ch sp, ch 3, dc in each st and in each ch sp across, turn (12 dc).

Row 17: Ch 1, sc in first st, (ch 1, skip next st, sc in next st) across leaving last st unworked, turn (6 sc, 5 ch sps).

Row 18: Repeat row 16 (10 dc).

Row 19: Ch 1, skip first st, sc

Continued on page 118

"Be Mine!" Appliqué

Designed by Nancy Hearne

Finished Size

Appliqué is 5½" x 6½".

Materials

- ❍ Size 20 crochet cotton — 125 yds. each cream and red
- ❍ No. 11 steel crochet hook or size needed to obtain gauge

Gauge

5 mesh = 1"; 11 dc rows = 2".
Notes: For **puff stitch (puff st),** yo, insert hook in next ch or sp, yo, jpull up long lp, (yo, insert hook in same sp, yo, pull up long lp) 4 times, yo, draw through all 11 lps on hook, ch1.

For **beginning puff st increase (beg puff st inc),** ch 5, puff st in 5th ch from hook, dc in next st.

For **mesh,** ch 2, skip next 2 chs or dc, dc in next dc.

For **ending puff st increase (end puff st inc),** (yo, insert hook in same st as last st made, yo, draw lp through) 5 times; to make one ch, yo, draw through one lp on hook, yo, draw through all 11 lps on hook, ch 1, yo, insert hook in ch made at base of puff st just made, yo, draw lp through; to make one ch, yo, draw through one lp on hook; (yo, draw through 2 lps on hook) 2 times.

For **block,** dc in each of next 3 sts or chs.

For **beginning puff st block (beg puff st block),** ch 3,

puff st in top of next puff st or in next ch-2 sp, dc in next dc.

For **puff st block,** puff st in top of next puff st or in next ch-2 sp, dc in next dc.

For **beginning decrease (beg dec),** sl st in first 4 sts.

For **end decrease (end dec),** leave last block unworked.

All mesh and puff st blocks are worked in cream, all blocks are worked in red.

Appliqué

Row 1: Starting at **bottom point,** with cream, ch 6, puff st in 5th ch from hook, dc in last ch, turn (1 puff st, block).

Rows 2-11: Work according to graph across, turn.

Note: When changing colors (see page 158), **do not** carry letter color across more than 3 sts. Use a separate ball of crochet cotton for each section. Fasten off letter color when no longer needed.

Rows 12-22: Work according to graph across, changing colors as indicated, turn.

Row 23: Work according to graph across, turn.

Row 24: For **first side,** work according to graph leaving remaining sts unworked, turn.

- ✕ = Beg Dec
- ● = End Dec
- ◈ = Beg Puff St Block
- ◆ = Puff St Block
- ▽ = Beg Puff St Inc
- ▼ = End Puff St Inc
- ⬛ = Red Block
- ⬜ = Mesh

Rows 25-26: Work according to graph across, turn. At end of last row, fasten off.

Row 24: For **2nd side,** skip next puff st on row 23, join with sl st in next dc, work according to graph, turn.

Rows 25-26: Work according to graph across, turn. At end of last row, fasten off.

Border

Notes: For **beginning V-st (beg V-st),** ch 6, dc in same ch.

For **V-st,** (dc, ch 3, dc) in end of next row or in next st.

For **picot,** ch 3, sl st in 3rd ch from hook.

Rnd 1: Working around entire outer edge, join red with sl st in top right-hand corner dc, ch 6, dc in same st, skipping center dc on row 23, V-st in each dc and in end of each row around with V-st in tip, join with sl st in 3rd ch of ch-6.

Rnd 2: Beg V-st, picot, (V-st in next sp between V-sts, picot) around, join, fasten off. ●

Egg Ornaments

Designed by Alice Heim

Finished Size

Egg No. 1 is 2¾" x 4".
Egg No. 2 is 2½" x 3½".
Egg No. 3 is 2½" x 3½".

Materials For Egg No. 1

- ○ Size 12 pearl cotton —
  100 yds. white
- ○ One skein green raffia straw
- ○ 2½" x 4" Styrofoam® egg
- ○ Shallow bowl
- ○ Craft glue or hot glue gun
- ○ Tapestry needle
- ○ No. 10 steel crochet hook or
  size needed to obtain gauge

Materials For Egg No. 2

- ○ Size 20 crochet cotton —
  75 yds. white
- ○ One skein pink raffia straw
- ○ 1⅞" x 2¾" Styrofoam® egg
- ○ Shallow bowl
- ○ Craft glue or hot glue gun
- ○ Tapestry needle
- ○ No. 7 steel crochet hook or
  size needed to obtain gauge

Materials For Egg No. 3

- ○ Size 30 crochet cotton — 75
  yds. white
- ○ One skein lavender raffia straw
- ○ 1⅞" x 2¾" Styrofoam® egg
- ○ Shallow bowl
- ○ Craft glue or hot glue gun
- ○ Tapestry needle
- ○ No. 13 steel crochet hook or
  size needed to obtain gauge

Gauges

Rnds 1-5 of Egg No. 1 = 1⅞"
across. Rnds 1-3 of Egg No. 2 =
1¾" across. For Egg No. 3, 15
dc sts = 1"; 5 dc rows = 1".

EGG NO. 1

Preparation
Note: One skein of raffia straw
covers several eggs.
Fill shallow bowl with a few
tablespoons of water. Open
raffia skein per package instructions, pass through bowl
to dampen and gently open to
full width. Holding one end of
raffia against bottom, wrap
around egg from one end to
the other, overlapping the
sides and crossing at the top
until entire egg is covered.
Cut raffia and pin end to egg;
glue in place when dry.

Cover
Rnd 1: Starting at **bottom,** ch
7, dc in 7th ch from hook, ch
3, (dc in same ch, ch 3) 4
times, join with sl st in 3rd ch
of ch-6 (6 dc, 6 ch-3 sps).

Rnd 2: Ch 1, sc in first st, ch 4,
sc in next ch-3 sp, (ch 4, sc in
next st, ch 4, sc in next ch-3
sp) around; to **join,** ch 2, hdc
in first sc (12 sc, 12 ch sps).

Notes: For **triple treble
(tr tr),** yo 4 times, insert
hook in next st, yo, draw lp
through, (yo, draw through 2
lps on hook) 5 times.

For **picot,** sl st in 4th ch from
hook.

Rnd 3: Ch 1, sc around joining
hdc, ch 9, picot, (ch 5, sc in
next ch-4 sp, ch 9, picot)
around; to **join,** tr tr in first sc
(25 ch sps).

Rnd 4: Ch 1, sc around joining
tr tr, ch 4, sc in next ch-5 sp,
ch 8, skip next picot, (sc in
next ch-5 sp, ch 4, sc in next
ch-5 sp, ch 8, skip next picot)
around, join with sl st in first sc
(12 ch-8 sps, 12 ch-4 sps).

Rnd 5: Sl st in next ch-4 sp, ch
4, 2 tr in same sp, ch 2, sc in
next ch-8 sp, ch 2, (3 tr in next
ch-4 sp, ch 2, sc in next ch-8
sp, ch 2) around, join with sl st
in top of ch-4 (36 tr, 24 ch-2
sps, 12 sc).

Rnd 6: Sl st in next tr, ch 1, sc in
same st, (ch 10, skip next tr, sc
in next sc or in next tr) around;
to **join,** ch 5, tr tr in first sc
(24 ch sps).

Rnd 7: Ch 1, sc around joining
tr tr, (ch 7, sc in next ch sp)
around; to **join,** ch 3, tr in
first sc.

Rnds 8-24: Ch 1, sc around
joining tr, (ch 7, sc in next ch
sp) around, join as before.

Rnd 25: Ch 1, sc around joining
tr, ch 22, (sc in next ch sp, ch
22) around, join with sl st in
first sc, fasten off.

Insert egg into Cover large end first.
With tapestry needle, weave separate piece crochet cotton through
ch 22 lps, pull tight to close
opening, tie into knot to secure.

Continued on page 106

Egg Ornaments
Continued from page 105

EGG NO. 2

Preparation
Work same as Egg No. 1 Preparation on page 105.

Cover
Rnd 1: Starting at **bottom,** ch 10, sl st in first ch to form ring, ch 3, 2 dc in ring, ch 3, (3 dc in ring, ch 3) 5 times, join with sl st in top of ch-3 (18 dc, 6 ch-3 sps).

Rnd 2: Ch 3, dc in same st, dc in next dc, 2 dc in next dc, ch 3, skip next ch-3 sp, (2 dc in next dc, dc in next dc, 2 dc in next dc, ch 3, skip next ch-3 sp) around, join (30 dc, 6 ch-3 sps).

Rnd 3: Ch 3, dc in same st, (*dc in next dc, ch 3, skip next dc, dc in next dc, 2 dc in next dc, ch 3, skip next ch-3 sp*, 2 dc in next dc) 5 times; repeat between **, join (36 dc, 12 ch-3 sps).

Rnd 4: Sl st in each of next 2 sts, sl st in first ch-3 sp, ch 3, 2 dc in same sp, ch 3, (3 dc in next ch-3 sp, ch 3) around, join with sl st in top of ch-3 (36 dc, 12 ch-3 sps).

Rnd 5: Sl st in each of next 2 sts, sl st in first ch-3 sp, ch 3, 2 dc in same sp, (ch 3, 3 dc in next ch-3 sp) around; to **join,** ch 1, hdc in top of ch-3.

Rnd 6: Ch 1, sc around joining hdc, ch 5, 3 dc in next ch-3 sp, ch 5, (sc in next ch-3 sp, ch 5, 3 dc in next ch-3 sp, ch 5) around, join with sl st in first sc (18 dc, 12 ch-5 sps, 6 sc).

Rnd 7: Ch 7, 3 dc in next ch-5 sp, dc in each of next 3 dc, 3 dc in next ch-5 sp, ch 3, (tr in next sc, ch 3, 3 dc in next ch-5 sp, dc in each of next 3 dc, 3 dc in next ch-5 sp, ch 3) around, join with sl st in 4th ch of ch-7 (54 dc).

Rnd 8: Sl st in next ch sp, ch 3, 2 dc in same sp, (*dc in each of next 3 dc, ch 3, skip next 3 dc, dc in each of next 3 dc, 3 dc in next ch sp, ch 3, skip next tr*, 3 dc in next ch sp) 5 times; repeat between **, join with sl st in top of ch-3.

Rnd 9: Ch 3, dc in each of next 2 dc, (*ch 3, skip next 3 dc, 3 dc in next ch-3 sp, ch 3, skip next 3 dc, dc in each of next 3 dc, ch 3, skip next ch-3 sp*, dc in each of next 3 dc) 5 times; repeat between **, join.

Rnd 10: Ch 3, dc in each of next 2 dc, (*3 dc in next ch-3 sp, ch 3, skip next 3 dc, 3 dc in next ch-3 sp, dc in each of next 3 dc, ch 3, skip next ch-3 sp*, dc in each of next 3 dc) 5 times; repeat between **, join.

Rnd 11: Ch 5, skip next 2 dc, (*dc in each of next 3 dc, 3 dc in next ch-3 sp, dc in each of next 3 dc, ch 2, skip next 2 dc, dc in next dc, ch 2, skip next ch-3 sp*, dc in next dc, ch 2, skip next 2 dc) 5 times; repeat between **, join with sl st in 3rd ch of ch-5.

Rnd 12: Ch 5, skip next ch-2 sp, [*dc next 2 dc tog, dc in next 5 dc, dc next 2 dc tog, ch 2, skip next ch-2 sp], (dc in next dc, ch 2, skip next ch-2 sp) 2 times; repeat from * 4 more times; repeat between [ ], dc in next dc, ch 2, skip last ch-2 sp, join.

Rnd 13: Ch 5, skip next ch-2 sp, [*dc next 2 dc tog, dc in each of next 3 dc, dc next 2 dc tog, ch 2, skip next ch-2 sp], (dc in next dc, ch 2, skip next ch-2 sp) 2 times; repeat from * 4 more times; repeat between [ ], dc in next dc, ch 2, skip last ch-2 sp, join.

Insert egg into Cover, large end first.

Rnd 14: Ch 5, skip next ch-2 sp, [*dc next 2 dc tog, dc in next dc, dc next 2 dc tog, ch 2, skip next ch-2 sp], (dc in next dc, ch 2, skip next ch-2 sp) 2 times; repeat from * 4 more times; repeat between [ ], dc in next dc, ch 2, skip last ch-2 sp, join.

Rnd 15: Ch 5, skip next ch-2 sp, [*dc next 3 dc tog, ch 2, skip next ch-2 sp], (dc in next dc, ch 2, skip next ch-2 sp) 2 times; repeat from * 4 more times; repeat between [ ], dc in next dc, ch 2, skip last ch-2 sp, join.

Rnd 16: Ch 5, skip next ch-2 sp, (dc in next dc, ch 2, skip next ch-2 sp) around, join.

Rnd 17: Sl st in next ch-2 sp, ch 4, tr in each ch-2 sp around, join with sl st in top of ch-4, fasten off.

EGG NO. 3

Preparation
Work same as Egg No. 1 Preparation on page 105.

Cover
Notes: For **mesh,** ch 2, skip next 2 dc or chs, dc in next dc.

For **block,** dc in each of next 3 dc, **or,** 2 dc in next ch sp, dc in next dc.

For **beginning mesh (beg mesh),** ch 5, skip next 2 chs, dc in next dc. Ch 5 counts as dc and ch-2.

For **beginning block (beg block),** ch 3, dc in each of next 3 dc.

Row 1: Ch 51, dc in 4th ch from hook, dc in each of next 2 chs, (ch 2, skip next 2 chs, dc in next ch) 13 times, dc in each of next 3 chs, ch 2, skip next 2 chs, dc in last ch, turn (14 mesh, 2 blocks).

Row 2-10: Work according to graph, turn.

Rows 11-30: Repeat rows 1-10 of graph consecutively, turn.

Rows 31-36: Repeat rows 1

and 2 of graph alternately, turn. At end of last row, leaving 8" for sewing, fasten off. Sew first and last rows together.

Trims
Rnd 1: Working in ends of rows, join with sc in first row, sc in same row, 2 sc in each row around, join with sl st in first sc (72 sc).
Rnd 2: Ch 1, sc in first st, ch 14, skip next 5 sts, sc in next st, ch 14, skip next 5 sts, (sc in next st, ch 14, skip next 4 sts) around, join, fasten off (14 ch lps).
Repeat on opposite side. Insert egg into cover.
With tapestry needle, weave separate strand crochet cotton through ch lps of one Trim, pull tight to close, secure. Repeat on opposite Trim. •

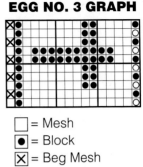

EGG NO. 3 GRAPH

☐ = Mesh
⬛ = Block
☒ = Beg Mesh
☐○ = Beg Block

Floral Lid Covers
Continued from page 96

Continued from page 96

next st, ch 3) around, join, fasten off.

Leaves
Note: For **beginning shell (beg shell),** ch 3, (dc, ch 2, 2 dc) in same st or sp.
For **shell,** (2 dc, ch 2, 2 dc) in next st or ch sp.
Rnd 1: With No. 7 hook and green bedspread cotton, ch 6, sl st in first ch to form ring, ch 5, (dc in ring, ch 2) 11 times, join with sl st in 3rd ch of ch-5 (12 dc, 12 ch sps).
Rnd 2: Sl st in next ch sp, beg shell, shell in each ch sp around, join with sl st in top of ch-3 (12 shells).
Rnd 3: Sl st in next st, sl st in next ch sp, beg shell, shell in ch sp of each shell around, join.
Rnd 4: Sl st in next st, sl st in next ch sp, beg shell, ch 1, (shell in next shell, ch 1) around, join.
Rnd 5: Sl st in next st, sl st in next ch sp, beg shell, ch 1, sc in next ch-1 sp, ch 1, (*shell in next shell, ch 1, sc in next ch-1 sp, ch 1) around, join, fasten off.
Tack to rnds 1-3 of Cover.

Flower
Row 1: With No. 7 hook and purple bedspread cotton, ch 20, dc in 4th ch from hook, (ch 1, skip next ch, 2 dc in next ch) across, turn (18 dc, 8 ch-1 sps).
Row 2: Sl st in sp between first 2 dc, *(dc, 5 tr, dc) in next ch-1 sp, sl st in sp between next 2 dc; repeat from * across, leaving 8" for sewing, fasten off.
Roll into flower shape, tack in place.
For **center,** with No. 7 hook and yellow bedspread cotton, ch 3, 2 dc in 3rd ch from hook, sl st in same ch, fasten off.
Tack to middle of Flower.
Center and sew Flower over Leaves. •

Yuletide Pot Holder

Designed by Isabelle Wolters

Finished Size

Pot holder is 7" square not including hanger.

Materials

- ○ 100% cotton 4-ply yarn — 2½ oz. white, small amount each green, red and yellow
- ○ Small amount gold embroidery floss
- ○ Tapestry needle
- ○ G crochet hook or size needed to obtain gauge

Gauge

4 sc = 1"; 4 sc rows = 1".

Front

Notes: When changing colors (see page 158), always drop yarn to wrong side of work. Work over dropped color across to next section of same color. Fasten off colors when no longer needed.

Row 1: With white, ch 26, sc in 2nd ch from hook, sc in each ch across, turn (25 sc).

Rows 2-27: Ch 1, sc in each st across changing colors according to graph, turn. At end of last row, **do not turn.**

Rnd 28: Working around outer edge, ch 1, sc in end of each row and in each st around with 3 sc in each corner, join with sl st in first sc, fasten off.

Border

Row 1: Repeat same row of Front.

Rows 2-27: Ch 1, sc in each st across, turn. At end of last row, **do not turn.**

Rnd 28: Repeat same rnd of Front.

Finishing

1: With green, using Outline Stitch (see illustration), embroider tree trunk as shown in photo.
2: With yellow, using Outline Stitch, embroider garland using photo as a guide for placement.
3: With red, using French Knot (see page 159), embroider 10 sts randomly spaced around tree.
4: With double strands gold embroidery floss, using Straight Stitch (see page 159), embroider 3 stitches at top of tree as shown.
5: Holding Front and Back wrong sides together, matching sts, with 2 strands red held together, whipstitch around outer edge, working over sts of rnd 28 as shown.
6: For **hanger,** with white, ch 12, sl st in first ch to form ring, ch 1, 24 sc in ring, join with sl st in first sc. Leaving 6" for sewing, fasten off.

Sew to center top of Pot Holder. •

OUTLINE STITCH

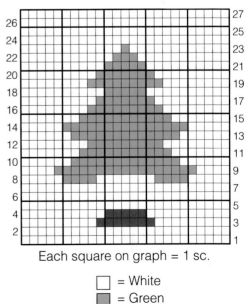

Each square on graph = 1 sc.

- ☐ = White
- ▨ = Green
- ▓ = Red

Christmas Pins

Designed by Dolly Dittler

Finished Size

All pins are 2¼" wide to 2¾" across.

Materials

- ❍ Worsted-weight yarn — small amount each red and white
- ❍ 1½" square piece of cardboard
- ❍ 1⅞" red paper clip
- ❍ Three ¾" pin backs
- ❍ Craft glue or hot glue gun
- ❍ G crochet hook or size needed to obtain gauge

Gauge

4 sts = 1"; 4 sc rows = 1"; 2 dc rows = 1".

Skate

Row 1: Working over paper clip across one long edge (see illustration), join white with sl st around clip, ch 2, 6 dc around clip; working over end, (dc, tr) around clip, turn (7 dc, 1 tr, 1 ch-2).

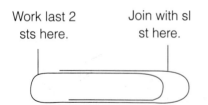

Work last 2 sts here.   Join with sl st here.

Row 2: Sl st in each of next 3 sts, ch 2, dc in same st, dc in next 4 sts leaving remaining sts unworked, turn (5 dc, 1 ch-2).

Row 3: Ch 2, dc in same st, dc in each st across, turn, fasten off.

Rnd 4: Working in rnds, leaving 6" end, join red with sc in **back lp** of first st, sc in **back lp** of each st across; **turn;** working across same row, sc in **front lp** of each st across, join with sl st in first sc.

Rnd 5: Ch 1, sc in first st, ch 3, (sc in next st, ch 3) around, join. Leaving 6" end, fasten off.

Tie 6" ends into a bow.

Glue pin back to center back of row 3.

Hat

Row 1: Starting at **top of Hat,** with red, ch 3, sc in 2nd ch from hook, sc in last ch, turn (2 sc).

Row 2: Ch 1, sc in each st across, turn.

Rows 3-9: Ch 1, sc in each st across to last st, 2 sc in last st, turn, ending with 9 sts in last row.

Row 10: Ch 1, sc in each st across, turn.

Rnd 11: Working in rnds, ch 1, sc in **back lp** of each st across; **turn,** working across same row, sc in **front lp** of each st across, join with sl st in first sc, fasten off (18).

Rnd 12: Join white with sl st in first st, ch 3, dc in each st around, join with sl st in top of ch-3, **turn.**

Rnds 13-14: Ch 3, dc in each st around, join. At end of last rnd, fasten off.

Fold last 2 rnds up for cuff.

Pom-Pom

For **pom-pom,** wrap white around cardboard 12 times, slide loops off cardboard, tie separate strand white around middle of all loops. Cut loops. Trim ends to ½". Sew to top of Hat.

Fold top of Hat down and sew to row 7.

Glue pin back to center back of row 10.

Mitten

Rnd 1: Starting at **palm,** with red, ch 4, sl st in first ch to form ring, ch 1, 8 sc in ring, join with sl st in first sc (8 sc).

Row 2: Ch 1, 2 sc in each of first 2 sts, (sc in next st, 2 sc in next st) around, join (13).

Row 3: Working in rows, ch 1, hdc in first st, (2 sc in next st, sc in next st) 4 times; for **thumb,** sl st in next st, ch 4, dc in 2nd ch from hook, dc in each of next 2 chs; for **wrist,** dc in same st as last sl st made, dc in each of next 2 sts, 2 dc in next st, dc in first ch-1, turn.

Row 4: Ch 1, sc in first 6 sts leaving remaining sts unworked, turn, fasten off.

Rnd 5: Working in rnds, join white with sl st in **back lp** of first st, ch 3, dc in **back lp** of each st across; **turn,** working across same row, dc in **front lp** of each st across, join with sl st in top of ch-3, **turn** (12 dc).

Rnd 6: Ch 3, dc in each st around, join, fasten off.

Fold last rnd up for cuff.

Glue pin back to bottom of rnd 2 on back of palm. •

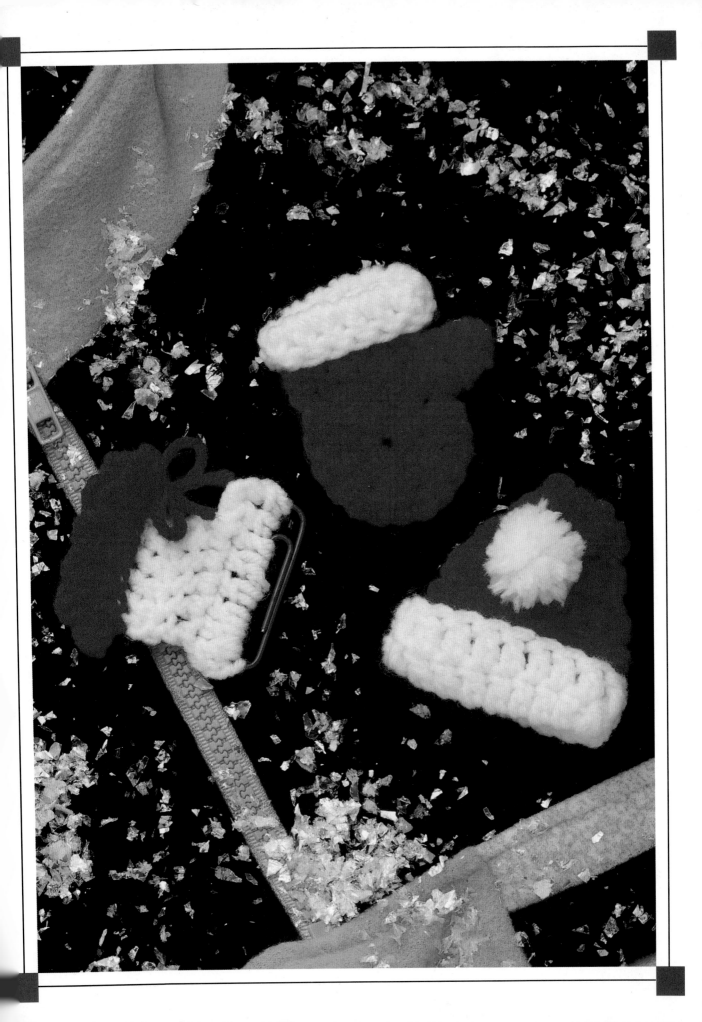

Halloween Cozies

Designed by Debra Yorston

Finished Size

Each Cozy is 4" tall x 2½" in diameter.

Materials For All Four

- ○ Worsted-weight yarn — 1½ oz. orange, 1 oz. each lavender and white, small amount each yellow, black, lime green and med. green
- ○ 4 black ½" flat buttons
- ○ 2 lime ⅝" flat buttons
- ○ One black ⅞" flat button
- ○ Tapestry needle
- ○ H crochet hook or size needed to obtain gauge

Gauge

7 sc = 2"; 4 sc rows = 1".

Ghost Cozy

NOTE: Do not join rnds unless otherwise stated. Mark first st of each rnd.

Rnd 1: With white, ch 2, 6 sc in 2nd ch from hook (6 sc).

Rnd 2: 2 sc in each st around (12).

Rnd 3: (2 sc in next st, sc in next st) around (18).

Rnd 4: (2 sc in next st, sc in each of next 2 sts) around (24).

Rnd 5: (2 sc in next st, sc in each of next 3 sts) around (30).

Rnd 6: Working this rnd in **back lps** only, sc in each st around.

Rnds 7-19: Sc in each st around. At end of last rnd, join with sl st in first sc.

Rnd 20: Ch 1; working left to right, **reverse sc** (see page 158) in each st around, join, fasten off.

Finishing

1: For **eyes,** with black, sew 2 black ½" buttons ⅛" apart over rnds 14-16 at a slight angle.

2: For **mouth,** with black, sew ⅞" black button centered below eyes over rnds 10-12.

3: With black, using Straight Stitch (see page 159), embroider **eyebrows** over each eye as shown in photo.

Pumpkin Cozy

With orange, work same as Ghost Cozy.

Finishing

1: For **eyes,** with black, sew 2 black ½" bottons ⅛" apart over rnds 13-15 at a slight angle.

2: With black, using Backstitch (see illustration), embroider **mouth** over rnds 10-11 as shown in photo.

3: Fold 6" piece of med. green in half, insert hook around center st between eyes on rnd 17, draw fold through, draw loose ends through fold, trim ends to ¾".

Monster Cozy

With lavender, work same as Ghost Cozy.

Finishing

1: For **eyes,** with lime, sew 2 lime buttons ⅛" apart over rnds 14-16 at a slight angle.

2: With black, using Backstitch (see illustration), embroider **mouth** over rnds 10-11 as shown in photo.

3: Fold 6" piece of orange in half, insert hook around st on one side of eyes, draw fold through, draw all loose ends through fold, trim ends to 2". Repeat on other side of eyes.

Candy Corn Cozy

Rnds 1-9: With yellow, repeat same rnds of Ghost Cozy. At end of last rnd, join wth sl st in first sc, fasten off.

Rnd 10: Join orange with sc in first st, sc in each st around.

Rnds 11-17: Sc in each st around. At end of last rnd, join with sl st in first sc, fasten off.

Rnd 18: Join white with sc in first st, sc in each st around.

Rnd 19: Sc in each st around, join with sl st in first sc.

Rnd 20: Repeat same rnd of Ghost Cozy. •

BACKSTITCH

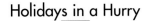

Turkey Kitchen Set

Designed by Patricia Hall

Finished Size

Pot Holder is 5¾" across.
Towel Holder is 3¼" x 7".
Turkey magnet is 2½" x 3¼".

Materials

- ○ Worsted-weight yarn —
  3 oz. yellow, 2 oz. brown,
  l oz. each orange, gold,
  and variegated, small
  amount each red and white
- ○ Size 10 bedspread cotton —
  small amount black
- ○ 2" plastic ring
- ○ One gold ⁷⁄₁₆" shank button
- ○ 3" magnetic strip
- ○ Craft glue or hot glue gun
- ○ Tapestry needle
- ○ B, D, F, G and H crochet
  hooks or size needed
  to obtain gauge

Gauge

With **H hook,** 7 sc = 2"; 4 sc
rows = 1"; 4 dc rows = 2¼".

POT HOLDER

Side (make 2)

Rnd 1: With H hook and yellow,
ch 4, sl st in first ch to form
ring, ch 3, 13 dc in ring, join
with sl st in top of ch-3 (14 dc).

Rnd 2: Ch 3, dc in same st, 2 dc
in each st around, join (28).

Rnd 3: Ch 3, dc in same st, dc
in next st, (2 dc in next st, dc
in next st) around, join (42).

Rnd 4: Ch 3, dc in same st, dc in
each of next 2 sts, (2 dc in next
st, dc in each of next 2 sts)

around, join, fasten off (56).

Edging

Rnd 1: Holding Sides wrong
sides together, matching
sts, working through both
thicknesses, with H hook and
yellow, join with sc in any st,
ch 5, skip next 3 sts, (sc in
next st, ch 5, skip next 3 sts)
around, join with sl st in first
sc; for **hanging loop,** ch
10, sl st in same st, fasten off
(14 ch-5 sps).

Rnd 2: Working in front of first
ch-5 sp, join orange with sc in
first skipped sc, ch 5; working
behind next ch-5 sp, sc in first
sc of next skipped 3-sc group,
ch 5; (working in front of next
ch-5 sp, sc in first sc of next
skipped 3-sc group, ch 5;
working behind next ch-5 sp,
sc in first sc of next skipped
3-sc group, ch 5) around,
join, fasten off.

Rnd 3: Working in front of first
ch-5 sp, join gold with sc in
next skipped sc on rnd 1, ch
5; working behind next ch-5
sp, sc in next sc of next
skipped 2-sc group on rnd 1,
ch 5; (working in front of next
ch-5 sp, sc in next sc of next
skipped 2-sc group on rnd 1,
ch 5; working behind next
ch-5 sp, sc in next sc of next
skipped 2-sc group on rnd 1,
ch 5) around, join, fasten off.

Rnd 4: Working in front of first
ch-5 sp, join brown with sc in
next skipped sc on rnd 1, ch 5;
working behind next ch-5 sp,
sc in next skipped sc on rnd 1,

ch 5; (working in front of next
ch-5 sp, sc in next skipped sc
on rnd 1, ch 5, working
behind next ch-5 sp, sc in next
skipped sc on rnd 1, ch 5)
around, join, fasten off.

TURKEY

(Make 3)

For **body,** with H hook and
brown, ch 4, sl st in first ch to
form ring, ch 3, 13 dc in ring,
join with sl st in top of ch-3,
do not fasten off (14 dc).

For **head,** ch 5, hdc in 3rd ch
from hook, 2 hdc in next ch,
hdc in last ch, sl st in next st
on body, fasten off.

Notes: For **treble cluster (tr-
cl),** *yo 2 times, insert hook
in same st, yo, draw lp
through, (yo, draw through 2
lps on hook) 2 times; repeat
from *, yo, draw through all 3
lps on hook.

For **double crochet cluster
(dc-cl),** (yo, insert hook in
same st, yo, draw lp through,
yo, draw through 2 lps on
hook) 2 times, yo, draw
through all 3 lps on hook.

For **tail feathers,** with G hook
and variegated, working in
back lps only, join with sl st in
next unworked st on body, (ch
4, tr-cl, ch 4, sl st) in same st, (sl
st, ch 4, tr-cl, ch 4, sl st) in each
of next 3 sts leaving remaining
sts unworked, fasten off.

For **wing feathers,** with F hook
and variegated, working in

Continued on page 118

Easter Egg Tissue Box

Designed by Beverly Mewhorter

Finished Size

Fits boutique-style tissue box.

Materials

○ Worsted-weight yarn —
  2½ oz. white, small amount
  each pink, lavender, green
  and yellow
○ Tapestry needle
○ H crochet hook or size
  needed to obtain gauge

Gauge

7 sc = 2"; 4 sc rows = 1".

Side (make 4)

Row 1: With white, ch 16, sc in
2nd ch from hook, sc in each
ch across, turn (15 sc).
Rows 2-21: Ch 1, sc in each st
across, turn. At end of last row,
fasten off.
Sew ends of rows on Sides together to form box.

Top

Row 1: Repeat same row of Side.
Rows 2-7: Ch 1, sc in each st
across, turn.
Row 8: Ch 1, sc in first 4 sts; for
opening, ch 7, skip next 7
sts; sc in last 4 sts, turn (8 sc,
1 ch-7 sp).
Row 9: Ch 1, sc in each st and
in each ch across, turn (15 sc).
Rows 10-16: Repeat row 2. At
end of last row, fasten off.
Easing to fit, sew Top to Sides.

Egg
(make one each green, lavender, yellow, pink)

Row 1: Ch 9, sc in 2nd ch from
hook, sc in each ch across,
turn (8 sc).
Row 2: Ch 1, 2 sc in first st, sc
in each st across to last st, 2 sc
in last st, turn (10).
Rows 3-6: Ch 1, sc in each st
across, turn.
Row 7: Ch 1, sc first 2 sts tog,
sc in each st across to last 2

sts, sc last 2 sts tog, turn (8).
Rows 8-9: Repeat row 3.
Rows 10-11: Repeat row 7
(6, 4).
Row 12: Repeat row 3.
Rnd 13: Working around outer
edge, ch 1, sc in each st and
in end of each row around
with 3 sc in each end of row
1, join with sl st in first sc,
fasten off.

Finishing

1: With indicated colors, using
Straight Stitch (see page 159),
embroider each Egg according
to Embroidery Diagrams on
page 119.
2: Cut 10" piece each of pink,
yellow, lavender and green.
Tie one piece into a bow
around each top corner. ●

Turkey Kitchen Set
Continued from page 115

front lps of same sts as tail feathers, join with sl st in first st, (ch 3, dc-cl, ch 3, sl st) in same st, (sl st, ch 3, dc-cl, ch 3, sl st) in each of next 3 sts, fasten off.

For **feet,** with F hook and orange, skip next st on body, join with sl st in next st, (ch 5, sl st in 2nd ch from hook, sl st in each of last 3 chs, sl st in same st as first sl st) 2 times, fasten off.

For **beak,** working on opposite side of ch-4 on head, with feathers toward you, with D hook and gold, join with sl st in 3rd ch, (ch 2, sl st in 2nd ch from hook, sl st in same ch as first sl st) 2 times, fasten off.

For **wattle,** with B hook and red, ch 4, (dc, ch 2, sl st) in 4th ch from hook, fasten off. Tack wattle below beak as shown in photo.

For **wing,** with G hook and variegated, ch 4, dc-cl in 4th ch from hook; for **picot,** ch 2, sc in top of last st made; ch 3, sl st in same ch as dc-cl, fasten off. Sew to body as shown.

With white, using French Knot (see page 159), embroider eye to Head as shown.

With bedspread cotton, using French Knot, embroider center of eye.

Sew one Turkey to center front of Pot Holder.

For Turkey magnet, glue magnetic strip to back of one Turkey.

TOWEL HOLDER

Ring Cover
Rnd 1: With H hook and yellow, work 32 sc around plastic ring (see illustration), join with sl st in first sc (32 sc).

SC OVER RING

Rnd 2: Ch 1, sc in first st, ch 5, skip next 3 sts, (sc in **front lp** of next st, ch 5, skip next 3 sts) 2 times, (sc in **both lps** of next st, ch 5, skip next 3 sts) around, join, fasten off (8 ch-5 sps).

Base
Row 1: With H hook and yellow, join with sc in **back lp** of 2nd st on rnd 1 of Ring Cover, sc in **back lp** of next 7 sts leaving remaining sts unworked, turn (8 sc).

Rows 2-28: Ch 1, sc in each st across, turn.

Row 29: Ch 1, sc in each of first 3 sts; for **buttonhole,** ch 2, skip next 2 sts; sc in each of last 3 sts, turn (6 sc, 1 ch-2 sp).

Row 30: Ch 1, sc in each st and in each ch across, fasten off (8 sc).

Ring Edging
Note: Work the following rnds in remaining lp or lps of rnd 1 on Ring Cover.

Rnd 1: Working in front of first ch-5 sp, join orange with sc in first skipped sc on rnd 1, ch 5; working behind next ch-5 sp, sc in first sc of next skipped 3-sc group, ch 5; (working in front of next ch-5 sp, sc in first st of next skipped 3-sc group, ch 5; working behind next ch-5 sp, sc in first sc of next skipped 3-sc group, ch 5) around, join, fasten off.

Rnd 2: Working in front of first ch sp, join gold with sc in next skipped sc on rnd 1 of Ring Cover, ch 5; working behind next ch sp, sc in first sc of next skipped 2-sc group on rnd 1 of Ring Cover, ch 5; (working in front of next ch sp, sc in first sc of next skipped 2-sc group on rnd 1 of Ring Cover, ch 5; working behind next ch sp, sc in first sc of next skipped 2-sc group on rnd 1 of Ring Cover, ch 5) around, join, fasten off.

Rnd 3: Working in front of first ch sp, join brown with sc in next skipped sc on rnd 1 of Ring Cover, ch 5; working behind next ch sp, sc in next skipped sc on rnd 1, ch 5; (working in front of next ch sp, sc in next skipped sc on rnd 1, ch 5; working behind next ch sp, sc in next skipped sc on rnd 1, ch 5) around, join, fasten off.

Sew button to center front of row 3 on Base. Fold bottom of Base up and insert button through buttonhole. Sew remaining Turkey over rows 19-28. •

Mistletoe Stocking
Continued from page 100

next 2 sts tog, (ch 1, skip next st, sc in next st) 3 times leaving last st unworked, fasten off.

Edging
Row 1: Working in remaining sts on row 11, join variegated with sl st in first st at top, ch 3, dc in next ch sp, (dc in next st, dc in next ch sp) 5 times, (hdc in next st, hdc in next ch sp) 5 times, (sc in next st, sc in next ch sp) 4 times, 2 sc in last st; working in ends of rows across top, 2 sc in each dc row and sc in each sc row across to row 19; for **toe shaping,** working in sts

across row 19, 2 sc in first st, hdc in next ch sp, hdc in next st, 3 dc in next ch sp, hdc in next st, hdc in next ch sp, 2 sc in last st; working in ends of rows across bottom, sc in each sc row and 2 sc in each dc row across to row 1; working in starting ch on opposite side of row 1; for **heel shaping,** 2 sc in first ch, hdc in each of next 3 chs, 2 dc in next ch, dc in next 4 chs, hdc in each of next 3 chs; sc in each of next 3 chs, hdc in

next 12 chs, dc in last 12 chs, **do not turn,** fasten off.

Row 2: Join burgundy with sc in first st, sc in each st across, fasten off.

Holding front and back wrong sides together, matching sts of row 2 on Edging, with burgundy, sew Front and Back together leaving top open.

Top Trim

Rnd 1: Working around top opening, join burgundy with sc in center back seam, sc in end of

each sc row and 2 sc in end of each dc row around, with sc in center front seam, join with sl st in first sc (46 sc).

Rnd 2: Ch 1, sc in first st, ch 2, skip next st, (sc in next st, ch 2, skip next st) around, join (23 ch sps).

Rnd 3: Ch 1, for **hanger,** (sc, ch 16, sc) in first st, (sc, ch 3, sc) in each ch sp around, join, fasten off.

Tie ribbon in bow around st on Stocking Front in upper left corner as shown in photo. •

Easter Egg Tissue Box
Continued from page 116

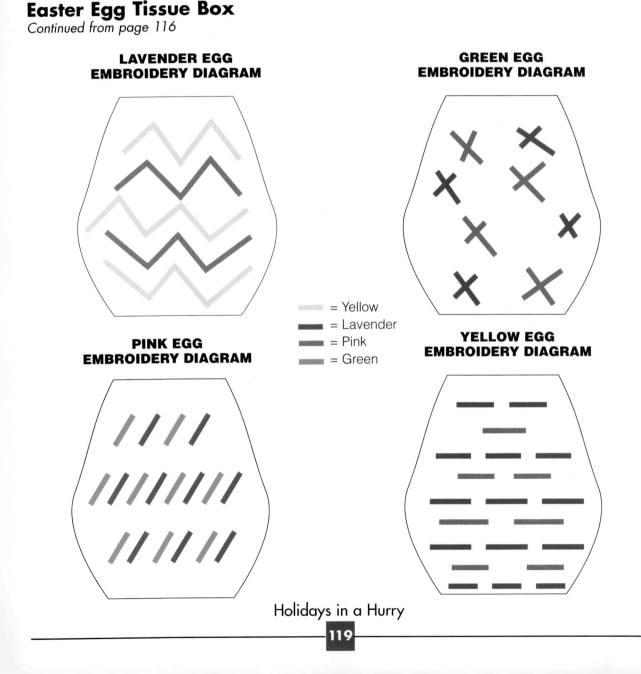

LAVENDER EGG EMBROIDERY DIAGRAM

GREEN EGG EMBROIDERY DIAGRAM

= Yellow
= Lavender
= Pink
= Green

PINK EGG EMBROIDERY DIAGRAM

YELLOW EGG EMBROIDERY DIAGRAM

Holidays in a Hurry

Easter Chicks Wreath

Designed by Beverly Mewhorter

Finished Size

Wreath is 10" across.

Materials

- Worsted-weight yarn — ½ oz. each yellow, peach and green, small amount orange
- 6 black 5-mm half round beads
- 4 assorted color 2½" plastic eggs
- 7 assorted color ½" plastic eggs
- 10" straw wreath
- Polyester fiberfill
- Craft glue or hot glue gun
- Tapestry needle
- H crochet hook or size needed to obtain gauge

Gauge

7 sc = 2"; 7 sc rows = 2".

Chick (make 3)
Head & Body Side (make 2)

Row 1: Starting at **bottom of Body,** with yellow, ch 6, sc in 2nd ch from hook, sc in each ch across, turn (5 sc).

Row 2: Ch 1, 2 sc in first st, sc in each of next 3 sts, 2 sc in last st, turn (7).

Rows 3-4: Ch 1, sc in each st across, turn.

Row 5: Ch 1, sc first 2 sts tog, sc in each of next 3 sts, sc last 2 sts tog, turn (5).

Row 6: Ch 1, sc first 2 sts tog, sc in next st, sc last 2 sts tog, turn (3).

Row 7: For **Head,** ch 1, 2 sc in first st, sc in next st, 2 sc in last st, turn (5).

Rows 8-9: Repeat row 3.

Row 10: Repeat row 6, fasten off. Holding Sides together, matching sts, with yellow, sew together, stuffing before closing.

Beak

With orange, ch 2, sc in 2nd ch from hook, fasten off.
Sew to center front of Head over row 8.

Wing

With yellow, ch 5, sc in 2nd ch from hook, dc in each of next 3 chs, fasten off.
Sew wide end of each Wing on each side of Body over rows 4-6.
For **eyes,** glue 2 half round beads centered above Beak ⅜" apart.

Grass

Row 1: With green, ch 30, sc in 2nd ch from hook, sc in each ch across, turn.

Row 2: Ch 1, (sc, ch 5, sc) in first st, *ch 5, (sc, ch 5, sc) in next st; repeat from * across, fasten off.

Bow

With peach, ch 100, sc in 2nd ch from hook, sc in each ch across to last ch, 3 sc in last ch; working on opposite side of ch, sc in each ch across to last ch, 2 sc in last ch, join with sl st in first sc, fasten off.
Fold into Bow. Wrap long strand of peach around middle of Bow several times; secure ends.

Finishing

1: Glue one 2½" egg in an upright position to center bottom of wreath on back edge.

2: For Hatching Chicks, open two 2½" eggs. Glue one Chick inside bottom half of each egg. Glue top half of same egg over top of Head on each Chick. Glue hatching Chicks to each side of first egg on wreath slightly to the front.

3: Glue remaining 2½" egg on its side to center front of wreath between hatching Chicks.

4: Glue remaining Chick to top of first upright egg.

5: Glue Grass across bottom front of wreath as shown in photo

6: Glue ½" eggs across bottom front of wreath 1½" apart as shown.

7: Glue Bow to top of wreath as shown. •

Basket of Pumpkins

Designed by Trudy Atteberry

Finished Size

Each Pumpkin is 3½" across.

Materials

- ○ Worsted-weight yarn —
  3 oz. orange
- ○ Size 3 crochet cotton —
  50 yds. green
- ○ Wooden basket
- ○ Natural raffia
- ○ 2 artificial sprigs of
  harvest bouquet
- ○ Polyester fiberfill
- ○ Tapestry needle
- ○ C and I crochet hooks or sizes
  needed to obtain gauge

Gauge

With **C hook and size 3
crochet cotton,** 6 sc = 1";
6 sc **back lp** rows = 1".
With **I hook and worsted-
weight yarn,** 3 sc = 1";
7 sc rows = 2".

Pumpkin (make 4)

Row 1: With I hook and
orange, ch 11, sc in 2nd ch
from hook, sc in each ch
across, turn (10 sc).

Rows 2-30: Ch 1, sc in each st
across, turn. At end of last
row, leaving long end for
sewing, fasten off.

Matching sts, sew first and last rows
together, weave through ends of
rows, pull to gather; secure.

Rnd 31: Working in ends of
rows across opposite edge,
join orange with sl st in first
row, ch 1, sc same row and
next row tog, (sc next 2 rows
tog) around, stuffing before
closing, join with sl st in first
sc. Leaving long end for
gathering, fasten off.

Weave end through rnd 31,
pull to gather, draw end
through top center to bottom
center of Pumpkin make
small st and draw back to
top pulling tightly to form
indentation; secure.

Stem

Row 1: With C hook and green,
ch 7, sc in 2nd ch from hook, sc
in each ch across, turn (6 sc).

Rows 2-8: Working these rows
in **back lps** only, ch 1, sc in
each st across, turn.

Row 9: Holding first and last
rows together, matching sts,
working through both thicknes-
es, ch 1, sl st in each st across,
do not turn.

Rnd 10: Working in ends of
rows, ch 1, 2 sc in each row
around, join with sl st in first sc.
Leaving long end for sewing,
fasten off.

Sew **back lps** of sts on last rnd
to top center of Pumpkin over
indentation.

Finishing

Fill basket almost full with raffia.
Insert one sprig of harvest
bouquet on each side. Fill
with Pumpkins. •

Little Chenille Bear

Designed by Michele Wilcox

Finished Size

Bear is 5¼" tall sitting.

Materials

- ○ Worsted-weight chenille yarn —2½ oz. tan
- ○ No. 3 pearl cotton — small amount brown
- ○ 16" red/white polka-dot 1" wired ribbon
- ○ Polyester fiberfill
- ○ Tapestry needle
- ○ H crochet hook or size needed to obtain gauge

Gauge

7 sc = 2"; 3 sc rows = 1".
Note: Use chenille yarn through-out unless otherwise stated.

Head

Note: Do not join rnds unless otherwise stated. Mark first st of each rnd.
Rnd 1: Starting at **muzzle,** ch 2, 6 sc in 2nd ch from hook (6 sc).
Rnd 2: 2 sc in each st around (12).
Rnds 3-4: Sc in each st around.
Rnd 5: 2 sc in each of first 6 sts, sc in last 6 sts (18).
Rnds 6-8: Sc in each st around.
Rnd 9: (Sc in next st, sc next 2 sts tog) around (12). Stuff.
Rnd 10: (Sc next 2 sts tog) around, join with sl st in first sc, leaving long end for sewing, fasten off (6).
Sew opening closed.

Ear (make 2)

Ch 2, 6 sc in 2nd ch from hook, join with sl st in first sc, fasten off.
Sew Ears over rnd 7 of Head 1¼" apart.

Finishing

1: With pearl cotton, using French Knot (see page 159), embroider eyes over top of rnd 4 spaced ¾" apart.
2: With pearl cotton, using Satin Stitch and Straight Stitch (see page 159), embroider **nose and mouth lines** over front of Head as shown in photo.

Body

Rnd 1: Starting at **bottom,** ch 2, 6 sc in 2nd ch from hook (6 sc).
Rnd 2: 2 sc in each st around (12).
Rnd 3: (Sc in next st, 2 sc in next st) around (18).
Rnd 4: (Sc in each of next 2 sts, 2 sc in next st) around (24).
Rnds 5-6: Sc in each st around.
Rnd 7: (Sc in each of next 2 sts, sc next 2 sts tog) around (18).
Rnd 8: Sc in each st around.
Rnd 9: (Sc in next st, sc next 2 sts tog) around (12).
Rnds 10-11: Sc in each st around. At end of last rnd, join with sl st in first sc, leaving long end for sewing, fasten off. Stuff.
Sew to bottom of Head.

Arm (make 2)

Rnd 1: Ch 2, 6 sc in 2nd ch from hook (6 sc).
Rnd 2: Sc in next 5 sts, 2 sc in next st (7).
Rnds 3-7: Sc in each st around. At end of last rnd, join with sl st in first sc, leaving long end for sewing, fasten off.
Flatten last rnd and sew over rnds 10 and 11 on each side of Body.

Leg (make 2)

Rnd 1: Ch 5, sc in 2nd ch from hook, sc in each of next 2 chs, 3 sc in last ch; working on opposite side of ch, sc in each of next 2 chs, 2 sc in last ch (10 sc).
Rnd 2: 2 sc in first st, sc in each of next 2 sts, 2 sc in each of next 3 sts, sc in each of next 2 sts, 2 sc in each of last 2 sts (16).
Rnd 3: Sc in each st around.
Rnd 4: Sc in each of first 3 sts, (sc next 2 sts tog) 4 times, sc in last 5 sts (12).
Rnd 5: Sc in each of first 2 sts, (sc next 2 sts tog) 3 times, sc in last 4 sts (9).
Rnds 6-8: Sc in each st around. At end of last rnd, join with sl st in first sc, leaving long end for sewing, fasten off. Stuff.
Flatten last rnd and sew over rnds 5 and 6 on each side of Body so Bear is sitting.
Tie ribbon into a bow around neck. •

Chapter Five

Holidays
Room by
Room

Taking a step-by-step tour
of your home will make it easier
to pick just the right spot to
add a crocheted home decor
accent. Create a focal point
and conversation piece
uniquely expressed through
your needlework.

Kitchen Flowers

Designed by Donna Piglowski

Finished Sizes

Flowerpot is 8" x 8½".
Wild Rose is 7" across.

Materials

○ Worsted-weight yarn — 4 oz. white, small amount each yellow, lt. pink, med. pink, and dk. pink, lt. green and dk. green and orange
○ Tapestry needle
○ G afghan hook and F crochet hook or size needed to obtain gauge

Gauge

With **G afghan hook,** 4 afghan sts = 1"; 4 afghan st rows = 1".

Flowerpot
Side (make 2)

Row 1: With afghan hook and white, ch 29; leaving all lps on hook, insert hook in 2nd ch from hook, yo, draw lp through, (insert hook in next ch, yo, draw lp through) across, **do not turn; to work sts off hook,** yo, draw through one lp on hook (see illustration a), (yo, draw through 2 lps on hook) across leaving one lp on hook at end of row (see illustration b)(29 vertical bars).

Row 2: For **afghan st,** skip first vertical bar, *insert hook under next vertical bar (see illustration c), yo, draw lp through; repeat from * across to last vertical bar; for **last**

st, insert hook under last bar and st directly behind it (see illustration d), yo, draw lp through; work sts off hook.

Rows 3-28: Work in afghan st.

Rnd 29: With F hook, skip first vertical bar, sc in each vertical bar across, ch 2, evenly sp 29 sc across ends of rows, ch 2; working in starting ch on opposite side of row 1, evenly sp 29 sc across, ch 2, evenly space 29 sc across ends of rows, join with sl st in first sc, fasten off.

With Cross-stitch (see illustration), embroider one Side according to Flowerpot Embroidery Diagram.

CROSS STITCH OVER AFGHAN STITCH ILLUSTRATION

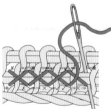

Border

Rnd 1: Holding Sides wrong sides together with embroidered Side facing you, join yellow with sc in any st, sc in each st around with (sc, c h 1, sc) in each ch-2 sp, join with sl st in first sc, fasten off.

Rnd 2: Join white with sc in any st; working from left to right, **reverse sc** (see page 159) in each sc and ch-1 sp around, join as before. Fasten off.

For **hanging loop,** with white, ch 10, fasten off.
Sew to back of pot holder.

AFGHAN STITCH ILLUSTRATIONS

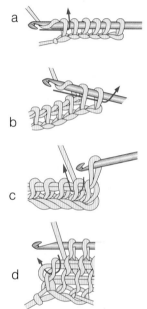

Wild Rose
Side (make 2)

Row 1: With afghan hook and white, ch 14, leaving all lps on hook, insert hook in 2nd ch from hook, yo, draw lp through, (insert hook in next ch, yo, draw lp through) across, **do not turn; to work sts off hook,** yo, draw through one lp on hook (see illustration a), (yo, draw through 2 lps on hook) across leaving one lp on hook at end of row (see illustration b)(14 vertical bars).

Rows 2-6: Insert hook between

Continued on page 130

Kitchen Flowers

Continued from page 129

first 2 vertical bars, yo, draw through, *insert hook under next vertical bar (see illustration c), yo, draw lp through; repeat from * across to last vertical bar, insert hook between last 2 vertical bars, yo, draw through; for **last st,** insert hook under last bar and st directly behind it (see illustration d), yo, draw lp through; work sts off hook.

Rows 7-18: Repeat row 2 of Flowerpot Side.

Rows 19-23: Skip first vertical bar, insert hook under next 2 vertical bars, yo, draw through, (insert hook under next vertical bar, yo, draw lp through) across to last 2 bars, insert hook under last 2 vertical bars, yo, draw through; work sts off hook, ending with 14 vertical bars.

Rnd 24: With F hook, skip first vertical bar, 3 hdc in next bar, sc in each vertical bar across with 3 hdc in last bar, *skip first row, sc in end of next 5 rows, 3 hdc in next row, sc in next 9 rows, 3 hdc in next row, sc in next 5 rows, skip last row*; working in starting ch on opposte side of row 1, 3 hdc in next ch, sc in next 4 chs, skip next ch, sc in each of next 2 chs, skip next ch, sc in next 4 chs, 3 hdc in next ch; repeat between **, join with sl st in top of first hdc, fasten off.

Finishing

With cross-stitch (see illustration), embroider one Side according to Wild Rose Embroidery Diagram.

Holding Sides wrong sides together with embroidered Side facing you; with F hook and dk. pink, join with sc in center st at top; for **hanging loop,** ch 8, sc in same st, sc in each st around with (hdc, 2 dc, hdc) in center st of each 3 hdc group, join with sl st in first sc, fasten off. •

FLOWERPOT EMBROIDERY DIAGRAM

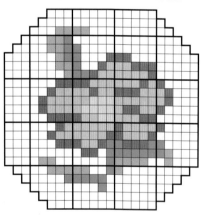

- ☐ = Med. Pink
- ☐ = Lt. Green
- ☐ = Lt. Pink
- ☐ = Yellow
- ☐ = Dk. Green
- ☐ = Dk. Pink
- ☐ = Orange

WILD ROSE EMBROIDERY DIAGRAM

Delicate Bell Edging

Designed by Jeanne Knape

Finished Size

Edging is 1⅜" wide.

Materials

- ◯ Size 20 crochet cotton —
  60 yds. ecru (see Notes)
- ◯ Tapestry needle
- ◯ No. 10 steel crochet hook or
  size needed to obtain gauge

Gauge

8 dc = ½"; 1 shell row = ¼".

Notes: For **shell,** (3 dc, ch 2, 3
dc) in next ch sp.

For **picot,** ch 4, sl st in **front lp**
of dc just made.

This pattern takes 10 yds.

to make 2½" of Edging.

Edging

Row 1: Ch 8, shell in 8th ch
from hook, turn (1 shell).

Row 2: Ch 5, shell in ch sp of
next shell, ch 2, dc in 5th ch
of ch-7, turn.

Row 3: Ch 5, shell in next shell,
ch 2; for **bell,** 6 dc in ch-5 lp
on last row, turn.

Row 4: Ch 3, dc in same st, dc
in next 4 sts, 2 dc in last st of
bell leaving remaining sts
unworked, turn (8 dc).

Row 5: Ch 3, dc in same st, dc
in each st across with 2 dc in
last st, turn.

Row 6: Ch 3, dc in next 4 sts,
picot, dc in last 5 sts, ch 10,

shell in next unworked shell,
ch 2, dc in 3rd ch of ch-5, turn.

Row 7: Ch 5, shell in next
shell, turn.

Row 8: Ch 5, shell next shell, ch
2, dc in 3rd ch of ch-5, turn.

Rows 9-11: Repeat rows 3-5.

Row 12: Ch 3; to **join bells,**
sl st in first ch of ch-10; dc
in next 4 sts, picot, dc in last
5 sts, ch 10, shell in next
unworked shell, ch 2, dc in
3rd ch of ch-5, turn.

Repeat rows 7-12 to desired
length ending with row 11.

Final Row: Ch 3; to **join
bells,** sl st in first ch of ch-10;
dc in next 4 sts, picot, dc in
last 5 sts. Fasten off. •

Watermelon Place Mat and Coaster

Designed by Ruth Shepherd

Finished Sizes

Place Mat is 13½" square.
Coaster is 5" across.

Materials For One of Each

○ Size 10 bedspread cotton —
   218 yds. each green,
   red and white, small
   amount black
○ Tapestry needle
○ No. 8 steel crochet hook
   or size needed to
   obtain gauge

Gauge

Each Square = 1⅜" across.
Notes: For **corner shell,** (3 dc,
ch 3, 3 dc) in next st or sp.
For **beginning shell (beg
   shell),** ch 3, (2 dc, ch 2,
   3 dc) in same st.
For **shell,** (3 dc, ch 2, 3 dc)
   in next st or sp.
Place Mat and Coaster may
ruffle until blocked.

PLACE MAT

Square (make 37 white, 15 red and 9 green)
Rnd 1: Ch 6, sl st in first ch to
   form ring, ch 3, 2 dc in ring,
   ch 3, (3 dc in ring, ch 3) 3
   times, join with sl st in top of
   ch-3 (12 dc, 4 ch sps).
Rnd 2: Ch 3, dc in each of
   next 2 sts, corner shell in
   next ch sp, *dc in each of
next 3 sts, corner shell in
next ch sp; repeat from *
around, join, fasten off (12
dc, 4 corner shells).
Sew Squares together through
   back lps according to Place
   Mat Diagram on page 152.

Border
Rnd 1: Working around entire
   outer edge, join white with sl
   st in center dc on corner
   Square as indicated on diagram, beg shell, [(ch 1, skip
   next 4 dc, corner shell in
   next ch sp, ch 1, skip next 4
   dc, shell in next st) 2 times,
   *ch 1, skip next 4 dc on
   next Square, shell in next dc,
   ch 1, skip next 4 dc, shell in
   next ch sp, ch 1, skip next 4
   dc, shell in next dc; repeat
   from * 3 more times, ch 1,
   skip next 4 dc on next
   corner Square], ◊shell in
   next dc; repeat between [ ];
   repeat from ◊ around, join
   with sl st in top of ch-3,
   fasten off (68 ch-1 sps, 60
   shells, 8 corner shells).
Rnd 2: Join green with sl st in
   ch sp of first shell, beg shell,
   ch 1, sc in next ch-1 sp, ch
   1, *shell in ch sp of next
   corner shell or next shell, ch
   1, sc in next ch-1 sp, ch 1;
   repeat from * around, join
   with sl st in top of ch-3,
   fasten off (68 shells).
Rnd 3: Join red with sc in first
   shell, [ch 3, sc in next sc, (ch

1, 9 dc in next shell, ch 1,
sc in next sc) 3 times, *(ch
3, sc in next shell, ch 3, sc
in next sc) 2 times, ch 1, 9
dc in next shell, ch 1, sc in
next sc; repeat from * 3
more times, ch 3, sc in next
shell, ch 3, sc in next sc, ch
3], ◊sc in next shell; repeat
between [ ]; repeat from ◊
one more time, join with sl st
in first sc, fasten off.
With black, using Lazy Daisy
Stitch (see illustration on
page 152), embroider
seeds over red Squares
according to diagram.

COASTER

Square (make 4 green and one red)
Work same Place Mat Square.
   Sew Squares together through
   back lps according to Coaster
   Diagram on page 152.

Border
Rnd 1: Working around entire
   outer edge, join white with sl
   st in center dc on Square as
   indicated on diagram, beg
   shell, (ch 1, skip next 4 dc,
   shell in next ch sp, ch 1, skip
   next 4 dc, shell in next dc) 2
   times, ch 1, skip next 4 dc
   on next Square, *shell in
   next dc; (ch 1, skip next 4
   dc, shell in next ch sp, ch 1,

Continued on page 152

Lyric Tablecloth

Designed by Lucille LaFlamme

Finished Size

Tablecloth is 50" square.

Materials

○ Size 10 bedspread cotton — 3,384 yds. ecru
○ Tapestry needle
○ No. 9 steel crochet hook or size needed to obtain gauge

Gauge

Rnds 1-2 of Motif = 1¾" across. Each motif is 5½" across.

Motif No. 1

Rnd 1: Ch 5, sl st in first ch to form ring, ch 11, tr in ring, ch 11, (tr in ring, ch 7, tr in ring, ch 11) 3 times, join with sl st in 4th ch of first ch-11 (4 ch-11 lps, 4 ch-7 lps).

Rnd 2: Sl st in first ch-7 lp, ch 1, 9 sc in same lp, ch 3, sc in next ch-11 lp, ch 3, (sc in same lp, ch 3) 5 times, *9 sc in next ch-7 lp, ch 3, sc in next ch-11 lp, ch 3, (sc in same lp, ch 3) 5 times; repeat from * around, join with sl st in first sc (60 sc, 28 ch-3 sps).

Rnd 3: Sl st in next 4 sts, ch 1, sc in same st, ch 5, skip next 2 ch-3 sps, sc in next ch-3 sp, (ch 4, sc in next ch-3 sp) 2 times, ch 5, skip next 2 ch-3 sps, *sc in 5th sc of next 9-sc group, ch 5, skip next 2 ch-3 sps, sc in next ch-3 sp, (ch 4, sc in next ch-3 sp) 2 times, ch 5, skip next 2 ch-3 sps; repeat from * around, join (16 sc, 8 ch-5 sps, 8 ch-4 sps).

Rnd 4: Ch 1, sc in same st, ch 9, skip next ch-5 sp, sc in next ch-4 sp, ch 11, sc in next ch-4 sp, *ch 9, skip next ch-5 sp, sc in next sc, ch 9, skip next ch-5 sp, sc in next ch-4 sp, ch 11, sc in next ch-4 sp; repeat from * around to last ch-5 sp, skip last sp; to **join,** ch 5, tr in first sc (8 ch-9 lps, 4 ch-11 lps).

Rnd 5: Ch 7, sc in 3rd ch of next ch-9 lp, ch 11, (2 tr, ch 7, 2 tr) in 6th ch of next ch-11 lp, ch 11, *sc in 7th ch of next ch-9 lp, ch 7, sc in 3rd ch of next ch-9 lp, ch 11, (2 tr, ch 7, 2 tr) in 6th ch of next ch-11 lp, ch 11; repeat from * around; to **join,** sc in joining tr of last rnd (8 ch-11 lps, 8 ch-7 lps).

Rnd 6: Ch 5, sc in next ch-7 lp, ch 5, sc in same lp, ch 5, sc in next sc, ch 7, (2 tr, ch 5, 2 tr) in 9th ch of next ch-11 lp, ch 3, (2 tr, ch 5, 2 tr) in 4th ch of next ch-7 lp, ch 3, (2 tr, ch 5, 2 tr) in 3rd ch of next ch-11 lp, ch 7, *sc in next sc, ch 5, sc in next ch-7 lp, ch 5, sc in same lp, ch 5, sc in next sc, ch 7, (2 tr, ch 5, 2 tr) in 9th ch of next ch-11 lp, ch 3, (2 tr, ch 5, 2 tr) in 4th ch of next ch-7 lp, ch 3, (2 tr, ch 5, 2 tr) in 3rd ch of next ch-11 lp, ch 7; repeat from * around, join with sl st in joining sc of last rnd.

Rnd 7: Sl st in next 3 chs, ch 1, sc in same sp, (ch 5, sc in next ch-5 sp) 2 times, ch 7, skip next ch-7 lp, (2 tr, ch 5, 2 tr) in 3rd ch of next ch-5 sp, ch 3, skip next ch-3 sp, (2 tr, ch 5, 3 tr, ch 5, 2 tr) in next ch-5 sp, ch 3, skip next ch-3 sp, (2 tr, ch 5, 2 tr) in 3rd ch of next ch-5 sp, ch 7, skip next ch-7 lp, *sc in next ch-5 sp, (ch 5, sc in next ch-5 sp) 2 times, ch 7, skip next ch-7 lp, (2 tr, ch 5, 2 tr) in 3rd ch of next ch-5 sp, ch 3, skip next ch-3 sp, (2 tr, ch 5, 3 tr, ch 5, 2 tr) in next ch-5 sp, ch 3, skip next ch-3 sp, (2 tr, ch 5, 2 tr) in 3rd ch of next ch-5 sp, ch 7, skip next ch-7 lp; repeat from * around, join with sl st in first sc.

Rnd 8: Sl st in next 3 chs, ch 1, sc in same sp, ch 21, sc in next ch-5 sp, ch 9, skip next ch-7 lp, (2 tr, ch 5, 2 tr) in 3rd ch of next ch-5, ch 3, skip next ch-3 sp, (2 tr, ch 5, 2 tr) in 3rd of next ch-5, tr in 2nd tr of next 3-tr group, ch 7, sl st in top of tr just made, (2 tr, ch 5, 2 tr) in 3rd ch of next ch-5, ch 3, skip next ch-3 sp, (2 tr, ch 5, 2 tr) in 3rd ch of next ch-5, ch 9, skip next ch-7 lp, *sc in next ch-5 sp, ch 21, sc in next ch-5 sp, ch 9, skip next ch-7 lp, (2 tr, ch 5, 2 tr) in 3rd ch of next ch-5, ch 3, skip next ch-3 sp, (2 tr, ch 5, 2 tr) in 3rd ch of next ch-5, tr in 2nd tr of next 3-tr group, ch 7, sl st in top of tr just made, (2 tr, ch 5, 2 tr) in 3rd ch of next ch-5, ch 3, skip next ch-3 sp, (2 tr, ch 5, 2 tr) in 3rd ch of next ch-5, ch 9, skip next ch-7 lp; repeat from * around, join, fasten off (16 ch-5 sps, 8 ch-9 lps, 8 ch-3 sps, 4 ch-21 lps).

Continued on page 139

Vanity Hearts

Designed by Rosemary Walter

Finished Sizes

Frame is 8" across and holds
2½" x 3¼" picture;
Tray is 9" across;
Cosmetic Caddy is 9" tall.

Materials

- ○ Worsted-weight yarn — 8 oz. rose and 4 oz. white
- ○ 5¼ yds. white ¾" gathered eyelet lace
- ○ 117 white 3-mm. pearl beads
- ○ Scissors
- ○ White sewing thread
- ○ Sewing and tapestry needles
- ○ 4 sheets 7-mesh plastic canvas
- ○ E and H crochet hooks or sizes needed to obtain gauges

Gauges

With **E hook,** 5 sc sts = 1";
5 sc rows = 1". With **H
hook,** 7 sc = 2"; 7 sc
rows = 2".

FRAME

Heart Side (make 2)
Note: Use E hook unless otherwise stated.
Row 1: Starting at **tip,** with rose, ch 2, sc in 2nd ch from hook, turn (1).
Row 2: Ch 1, 3 sc in first st, turn (3).
Rows 3-12: Ch 1, 2 sc in first st, sc in each st across with 2 sc in last st, turn, ending with 23 sts in last row.
Row 13: Ch 1, sc in each st across, turn.
Rows 14-22: Repeat rows 3 and 13 alternately, ending with row 3 and 33 sts on last row.
Rows 23-28: Repeat row 13.
Row 29: Ch 1, sc first 2 sts tog, sc in each st across to last 2 sts, sc last 2 sts tog, turn (31).
Row 30: Repeat row 13.
Row 31: For **first side,** ch 1, sc first 2 sts tog, sc in next 12 sts leaving remaining sts unworked, turn (13).
Rows 32-35: Repeat row 29, ending with 5 sts in last row. At end of last row, fasten off.
Row 31: For **second side,** skip next 3 unworked sts on row 30, join rose with sc in next st, sc in each st across to last 2 sts, sc last 2 sts tog, turn (13).
Rows 32-35: Repeat same rows of first side.
Rnd 36: Working around outer edge; for **edging,** join rose with sc in center st of unworked sts on row 30, sc in each st and in end of each row around with 2 sc in each end of row 35 on first and second sides and 3 sc in tip, join with sl st in first sc, fasten off.
Rnd 37: Join white with sc in first st, sc in each st around with 2 sc in each corner and 3 sc in tip, join, **turn.** For **back,** fasten off.
Rnd 38: For **front,** working this rnd in **back lps,** ch 2, 2 hdc in same st, hdc in each st around with (hdc next 3 sts tog) at tip, join, fasten off.
Using front as pattern, cut one piece from plastic canvas.
Holding wrong side of crochet front to plastic canvas heart, fold rnd 38 over plastic canvas. With white, sew together, stitching through top of each hdc on rnd 38.
With white, using Straight Stitch (see page 159), embroider lattice pattern according to Embroidery Diagram.

EMBROIDERY DIAGRAM

Center Piece
With white, ch 60, sl st in first ch to form ring, ch 2, (hdc next 2 chs tog, hdc in next ch) 3 times, hdc in next 11 chs; repeat between ( ) 3 more times, hdc in next ch; repeat between ( ) 3 more times, hdc in next 11 chs; repeat between ( ) 3 more times, join with sl st in top of ch-2, fasten off.
Cut one piece plastic canvas 2½" x 3½", trim ½" from each corner diagonally. Trim

Continued on page 138

Vanity Hearts

Continued from page 137

picture to fit inside Center Piece.

Holding wrong side of Center Piece and plastic canvas together with picture between, with white, sew opposite side of starting ch on Center Piece around outer edge of plastic canvas. Sew 12" piece lace around outer edge on back, overlapping ends.

Sew Center Piece to front with upper edge at top point.

Sew one pearl to every other hdc on center piece and to intersection of lattice pattern stitches on front.

With white, matching stitches, sew heart back to heart front. Sew 25" piece lace around outer edge of heart back, overlapping ends.

TRAY

Base

Note: Use H hook unless otherwise stated.

Rows 1-35: Repeat same rows of Frame Heart Side.

Rnd 36: Repeat same rnd of Frame Heart Side, **do not fasten off.**

Rnd 37: Working this rnd in **back lps**; for **sides**, ch 1, sc in each st around, join.

Rnds 38-42: Working in **both lps**, repeat rnd 37. At end of last rnd, fasten off.

Rnd 43: For **trim**, join white with sc in any st, sc in each st around, join, **turn.**

Rnd 44: Repeat rnd 37, fasten off.

With white, sew rnd 44 over rnd 42 on outside.

Bottom Trim

Rnd 1: With bottom of heart facing you, working in **front lps** of rnd 36, join white with sc in any st, sc in each st around, join.

Rnd 2: Working this rnd in **back lps,** ch 1, sc in each st around, join, fasten off.

With white, sew rnd 2 over rnd 38 of sides.

For **sides**, cut two pieces plastic canvas 1" x 13" or length needed to fit around heart. With white, whipstitch (see illustration) short ends together. Using Tray base as pattern, cut one piece from plastic canvas. Whipstitch plastic canvas sides to plastic canvas base. Place plastic canvas pieces inside crocheted pieces, with white, tack plastic canvas sides to white trim of crocheted sides.

With white, using Straight Stitch (see page 159), embroider a cross pattern around sides between top and bottom edging as shown in photo. Sew pearl to center of each cross. Sew 31" piece lace to rnd 1 of Bottom Edging.

Liner

Rows 1-35: Repeat same rows of Frame Heart Side.

Rnd 36: Repeat same rnd of Frame Heart Side, **do not fasten off.**

Rnd 37: Working this rnd in **front lps**, ch 1, sc in each st around, join.

Rnd 38-41: Working in **both lps,** repeat rnd 37. At end of last rnd, fasten off.

Rnd 42: Join white with sc in any st, sc in each st around, join, fasten off.

Place inside Tray, sew to plastic canvas in corners and around outside edges.

Sew 27" piece lace to rnd 42 of Liner having lace upside down and on inside of Tray as shown.

COSMETIC CADDY

Note: Use H hook unless otherwise stated.

Heart Side (make 2)

Work same as Frame Heart Side on page 137. Increase lace measurement to 31" to fit around outer edge of Heart.

Box

Row 1: Starting at **bottom,** with rose, ch 17, sc in 2nd ch from hook, sc in each ch across, turn (16).

Rows 2-24: Ch 1, sc in each st across, turn.

Rnd 25: Working around outer edge, ch 1, sc in each st and in end of each row around with 3 sc in each corner.

Rnd 26: Working this rnd in **back lps**; for **sides**, sc in each st around.

Rnds 27-37: Working in **both lps,** repeat rnd 26. At end of last rnd, fasten off.

Rnd 38: Join white with sl st in any st, ch 3, dc in each st around, join with sl st in top of ch-3, fasten off.

For **bottom trim,** working in **front lps** of rnd 25, with bottom facing you, join white with sl st in any st, sl st in each st around, join with sl st in first sl st, fasten off.

For **base,** cut one piece plastic canvas 4⅝" x 6¾". For **sides,** cut two pieces 3½" x 6¾ and **for ends,** two pieces 3½" x 4⅝". Whipstitch pieces together to form box. Place plastic canvas box inside crocheted piece. Sew together in corners and around outside edges.

Fold rnd 38 to inside, tack to plastic canvas. Cut remaining lace in half. Sew one piece over rnd 38 around top of Box, sew last piece around sl st trim on bottom of Box.

Sew Heart to one long side of box, having bottom edges even as shown. •

WHIPSTITCH

Lyric Tablecloth
Continued from page 134

Motif Nos 2-81
Notes: For **joining ch-21 lp,** ch 10, sl st in ch-21 lp of next Motif, ch 10.

For **joining ch-5 sp,** ch 2, sl st in ch-5 sp of next Motif, ch 2.

For **joining ch-7 lp,** ch 3, sl st in ch-7 lp of next Motif, ch 3.

Join Motifs according to Joining Diagram in 9 rows of 9 Motifs each.

Rnds 1-7: Repeat same rnds of Motif No.1 on page 134.

Rnd 8: Repeat same rnd of Motif No. 1 using joining ch-21 lps, joining ch-5 sps and joining ch-7 lps when joining Motifs.

Border
Note: For **picot,** ch 5, sl st in top of last st made.

Join with sl st in any corner ch-7 lp, ch 4, (2 tr, picot, 3 tr) in same lp, [ch 7, sc in next ch-5 sp, picot, *ch 7, (3 tr, picot, 3 tr) in next ch-5 sp, ch 11, (2 sc, picot, 2 sc) in next ch-21 lp, ch 11, (3 tr, picot, 3 tr) in next ch-5 sp*, ◊ch 7, (3 tr, picot, 3 tr) in next ch-5 sp, ch 5, skip next 2 joining ch-7 lps, (3 tr, picot, 3 tr) in next ch- 5 sp; repeat between **; repeat from ◊ 7 more times, ch 7, sc in next ch-5 sp, picot, ch 7], •(3 tr, picot, 3 tr) in corner ch-7 lp; repeat between [ ]; repeat from • around, join with sl st in top of first ch-4, fasten off. •

JOINING DIAGRAM

| = Joining ch-7 lp | = Joining ch-5 lp | = Joining ch-21 lp

Motif

Crimson Tree Skirt

Designed by Katherine Eng

Finished Size

Tree Skirt is 13" wide. Fits up to 7" tree trunk.

Materials

○ Worsted-weight yarn — 7 oz. red, 3 oz. green and 2½ oz. blue
○ 4 blue ½" buttons
○ 3¼ yds. green ⅜" satin ribbon
○ Blue sewing thread
○ Sewing and tapestry needles
○ G crochet hook or size needed to obtain gauge

Gauge

3 dc = 1"; 9 dc rows = 5".

First Panel

Row 1: With red, ch 4, sc in 2nd ch from hook, sc in each of last 2 chs, turn (3 sc).

Row 2: Ch 1, sc in each st across, turn.

Row 3: Ch 3, dc in same st, dc in each st across with 2 dc in last st, turn (5 dc).

Row 4: Ch 3, dc in same st, dc in next st, ch 2, skip next st, dc in next st, 2 dc in last st, turn (6 dc, 1 ch-2 sp).

Row 5: Ch 3, dc in each st across to next ch-2 sp, ch 2, sc in next ch-2 sp, ch 2, dc in each st across, turn.

Row 6: Ch 3, dc in same st, dc in each st across to next ch-2 sp, ch 2, skip next 2 ch-2 sps, dc in each st across with 2 dc in last st, turn.

Rows 7-20: Repeat rows 5 and 6 alternately, ending with 22

dc and one ch-2 sp in last row.

Row 21: Ch 1, sc in first st, skip next st, 3 dc in next st, skip next st, sc in next st, skip next st, 5 dc in next st, skip next 2 sts, sc in next st, skip next st, (3 dc, ch 2, 3 dc) in next ch-2 sp, skip next st, sc in next st, skip next 2 sts, 5 dc in next st, skip next st, sc in next st, skip next st, 3 dc in next st, skip next st, sc in last st, fasten of (28 sts).

Rnd 22: Working in starting ch, on opposite side of row 1, join blue with sc in center ch, (sc, ch 2, sc) in next ch; working in ends of rows, ch 1, skip first row, sc in next row, (ch 2, sc in top of next row) 18 times; working across last row, (sc, ch 2, sc) in first st, ch 1, skip next st, (sc, ch 2, sc) in next st, ch 1, skip next st, *sc in next st, ch 2, skip next 2 sts, (sc, ch 2, sc) in next st, ch 2, skip next 2 sts, sc in next st*, ch 3, skip next 3 sts, (sc, ch 2, sc) in next ch sp, ch 3, skip next 3 sts; repeat between **, ch 1, skip next st, (sc, ch 2, sc) in next st, ch 1, skip next st, (sc, ch 2, sc) in last st; working in ends of rows, (sc in top of next dc row, ch 2) 18 times, sc in next sc row, ch 1, skip last row, (sc, ch 2, sc) in next ch on row 1, join with sl st in first sc, fasten off.

Rnd 23: Join green with sc in first st, ch 1, skip next st, (sc, ch 2, sc) in next corner ch-2 sp, ch 2, skip next st, sc in next st, (ch 2, skip next ch-2 sp, sc in next st) 18 times, ch 2, skip next st, (sc, ch 2, sc) in next corner ch-2 sp, sc in next st, ch

1, skip next ch-1 sp, (sc, ch 2, sc) in next ch-2 sp, ch 1, skip next st, *sc in next st, ch 2, skip next ch 2-sp, (sc, ch 3, sc) in next ch-2 sp, ch 2, skip next ch-2 sp, sc in next st* ch 3, skip next ch-3 sp, sc in next st, (sc, ch 3, sc) in next ch-2 sp, sc in next st, ch 3, skip next ch-3 sp; repeat between **, ch 1, skip next ch-1 sp, (sc, ch 2, sc) in next ch-2 sp, ch 1, skip next ch-1 sp, sc in next st, (sc, ch 2, sc) in next corner ch-2 sp, ch 1, skip next st, sc in next st, (ch 2, skip next ch-2 sp, sc in next st) 18 times, ch 1, skip next ch-1 sp, (sc, ch 2, sc) in next corner ch-2 sp, ch 1, skip last st, join, fasten off.

Next Panel

Rows/Rnd 1-22: Repeat same rows/rnds of First Panel.

Notes: For **joining ch sp,** ch 1, drop lp from hook, insert hook in corresponding ch-2 or ch-1 sp on previous Panel, draw dropped lp through, ch 1.

Join Panels across one long edge.

Rnd 23: Join green with sc in first st, ch 1, skip next st, (sc, ch 2, sc) in next corner ch-2 sp, ch 2, skip next st, sc in next st, (ch 2, skip next ch-2 sp, sc in next st) 18 times, ch 2, skip next st, (sc, ch 2, sc) in next corner ch-2 sp, sc in next st, ch 1, skip next ch-1 sp, (sc, ch 2, sc) in next ch-2 sp, ch 1, skip next st, *sc in next st, ch 2, skip next ch-2 sp, (sc, ch 3, sc) in next ch-2 sp, ch 2, skip next

Continued on page 149

Victorian Sleigh

Designed by Rosemary Walter

Finished Size

Sleigh is 5" tall.

Materials

- ○ Worsted-weight yarn —
  4 oz. white; 3 oz. rose
  and 2 oz. gray
- ○ 12" x 18" sheet stiff 7-mesh
  plastic canvas
- ○ 1⅔ yds. iridescent 3-mm
  strung beads
- ○ 1 yd. gray ¼" satin ribbon,
  1 yd rose ¼" satin ribbon
- ○ Sewing thread — gray,
  white and rose
- ○ Sewing and tapestry needles
- ○ E and F crochet hooks or sizes
  needed to obtain gauges

Gauges

With **E hook,** 5 sc sts = 1";
  5 sc rows = 1".
With **F hook,** 9 sc sts = 2";
  9 sc rows = 2".

Outside
Side (make 2)

Row 1: With F hook and white,
  ch 8, sc in 2nd ch from hook,
  sc in each ch across, turn (7).
Row 2: Ch 3, sc in 2nd ch from
  hook , sc in each ch and in
  each sc across, turn (9).
Row 3: Ch 1, sc in each st
  across, turn.
Rows 4-13: Repeat rows 2 and
  3 alternately, ending with 19
  sts in last row.
Row 14: Ch 1, sc in each st
  across to last 2 sts, sc last 2
  sts tog, turn (18).

Row 15: Repeat row 3.
Rows 16-26: Repeat rows 14
  and 3 alternately, ending with
  row 14 and 12 sts.
Row 27: Ch 1, sc first 2 sts tog,
  sc in each st across, turn (11).
Rows 28-32: Repeat rows 14
  and 27 alternately, ending
  with row 14 and 6 sts.
Rows 33-38: Repeat row 3.
Rows 39-46: Repeat rows 2
  and 27 alternately, ending
  with 10 sts in last row.
Row 47: Repeat row 14 (9).
Row 48: Ch 1, sc first 2 sts tog,
  sc in each st across to last 2
  sts, sc last 2 sts tog. For **first
  side,** turn; for **second side,
  do not turn** (7).
Rnd 49: Working around outer
  edge, ch 1, sc in each st and
  in end of each row around
  with 2 sc in each corner, join
  with sl st in first sc, fasten off.
Cut one piece from plastic
  canvas ¼" smaller than
  crocheted piece.

Center

Row 1: For **first side,** with
  right side facing you and
  working in **back lps,** with F
  hook and white, join with sc
  in top front corner as indicated on diagram on page 154,
  sc in each st across sides and
  bottom to top back corner,
  turn (70).
Rows 2-8: Ch 1, sc in each st
  across, turn. Fasten off at end
  of last row.
Row 1: For **second side,** with
  right side facing you and
  working in **back lps,** with F

hook and white, join with sc
  in top back corner as indicated on diagram, sc in each st
  across sides and bottom to
  front corner, turn (70).
Rows 2-8: Repeat same rows
  of first side.
With white, matching sts, sew
  first and second sides of
  Center pieces together across
  row 8. Cut one 3" x 15"
  piece from plastic canvas.

Inside
Side (make 2)

With E hook and rose, work
  same as Outside's Side.
  Do not cut plastic canvas
  when finished.

Center

With E hook and rose, working
  row 1 in **front lps,** work
  same as Outside's Center.

Runner (make 2)

Rnd 1: With F hook and gray,
  ch 65, dc in 4th ch from
  hook, dc in each ch across
  with 2 dc in last ch; working
  on opposite side of ch, dc in
  each ch across, join with sl st
  in top of ch-3.
Rnd 2: Ch 3, dc in each st
  around, join.
Cut ¾" x 13" strip of plastic
  canvas. Fold crocheted piece
  in half lengthwise, place
  plastic canvas inside.
Row 3: Working across one
  long edge and through
  both thicknesses, with plastic

Continued on page 154

Holiday Pillow

Designed by Francine Marlin

Finished Size

Pillow is 17" x 20".

Materials

- ○ Worsted-weight yarn —
  8 oz. each red and white
- ○ Woven acrylic sport yarn —
  5½ oz. green
- ○ Metallic gold braid
- ○ ½ yd. fabric
- ○ Polyester fiberfill
- ○ Sewing thread
- ○ Sewing and tapestry needles
- ○ I crochet hook or size
  needed to obtain gauge

Gauge

With **2 strands yarn held together,** 3 sc = 1"; 7 sc rows = 2".

Note: Work entire pattern with 2 strands yarn held together.

Front

Row 1: With white, ch 64, sc in 2nd ch from hook, sc in each ch across, turn (63 sc).

Rows 2-6: Ch 1, sc in each st across, turn.

Rows 7-56: Ch 1, sc in first 6 sts changing to red in last st made (see page 158), sc in each st across to last 6 sts changing to white in last st made, sc in last 6 sts, turn.

Rows 57-62: Ch 1, sc in each st across, turn. At end of last row, fasten off.

With 2 strands held together, using Cross Stitch (see illustration) and Straight Stitch (see page 159), embroider red section of Pillow according to graph on page 153.

CROSS STITCH

With 2 strands green, using Straight Stitch, embroider "MERRY CHRISTMAS!" centered below trees as shown in photo. With one stand gold metallic braid, using Straight Stitch, embroider an outline around the green stitched letters.

Back

Using Front as pattern, cut fabric piece ½" larger around outer edges. Fold ½" to inside and sew Back to Front, stuffing before closing.

Twisted Cord

Cut 2 strands red each 4 yds. long. With both strands held together, fold in half; tie ends in knot. Secure knot on a nail or door knob; place a pencil in fold and turn, twisting the yarn until it will twist back on itself when released. Fold twisted yarn in half holding ends together, release folded end and let yarn twist back on itself. Tie a separate piece of yarn tightly about 1" from each end; trim ends about ½" from knots.

Tie into bow and tack to Front corner of Pillow.

Tassell (make 2)

Cut 75 strands green each 14" long. Tie separate strand green tightly around middle of all strands; fold strands in half. Wrap another 20" strand around folded strands 2" from top of fold, covering ¼"; secure and hide ends inside Tassel. Trim all ends evenly.

Tie Tassels to ends of Cord. ●

Rows 4-6: Ch 2, dc bp around each of next 3 sts, dc fp around each of next 4 sts (dc bp around each of next 4 sts, dc fp around each of next 4 sts) across, turn.

Rows 7-9: Repeat row 2.

Rows 10-15: Repeat rows 4-9. At end of last row, **do not turn,** fasten off.

Row 16: Join red/green with sc in first st, sc in each st across, turn.

Row 17: Ch 1, sc in each st across, turn, fasten off.

Row 18: Join gold with sl st in first st, ch 3, dc in each st across, turn.

Rows 19-20: Repeat row 2. At end of last row, fasten off.

Rows 21-23: Repeat rows 16-18.

Rows 24-25: Repeat row 2.

Row 26: Ch 1, sc in first st, (ch 5, skip next 3 sts, sc in next st) across to last 3 sts, ch 5, skip next 2 sts, sc in last st, fasten off. With gold, sew ends of rows together.

Base

Row 1: With gold, ch 78, dc in 4th ch from hook, dc in each ch across, turn (76 dc).

Rows 2-12: Ch 3, dc in each st across, turn. At end of last row, fasten off.

To **join,** holding Base against row 1 of Sides, working through both thicknesses, join gold with sc in any st, sc in each st around working 2 sc in end of each dc row on Base, join with sl st in first sc, fasten off.

Poinsettia

Work same as Doily's Poinsettia on page 147. With gold, sew center of Poinsettia over rows 16 and 17 on one side of Box.

Finishing

Stiffen Box and Poinsettia according to manufacturer's instructions. Cover tissue box with foil. Shape crochet box over side of tissue box. Let dry completely.

For **extra support** (optional), cut plastic canvas as follows: For **sides,** cut two pieces each 23 x 61 holes. For **ends,** cut two pieces each 18 x 23 holes. For **base,** cut one piece 18 x 61 holes. With 4-ply yarn, whipstitch (see illustration) sides and ends and base together to form box. Place inside Card Box. •

WHIPSTITCH

Crimson Tree Skirt
Continued from page 140

ch-2 sp, sc in next st*, ch 3, skip next ch-3 sp, sc in next st, (sc, ch 3, sc) in next ch-2 sp, sc in next st, ch 3, skip next ch-3 sp; repeat between **, ch 1, skip next ch-1 sp, (sc, ch 2, sc) in next ch-2 sp, ch 1, skip next ch-1 sp, sc in next st; to **join Panels,** sc in next corner ch-2 sp, work joining ch sp, sc in same ch sp on this Panel, work joining ch sp, skip next st on this Panel, sc in next st, (work joining ch sp, skip next ch-2 sp on this Panel, sc in next st) 18 times, work joining ch sp, skip next ch-1 sp on this Panel, sc in next corner ch-2 sp, work joining ch sp, sc in same ch sp on this Panel, ch 1, skip last st, join, fasten off.

Repeat Next Panel 9 more times for a total of 11 Panels.

Edging

Working across long edges of back opening and around top of Panels in center of Skirt, join green with sl st in bottom corner ch-2 sp before long edge, ch 3, sl st in next st, (ch 2, skip next ch sp, sl st in next st) 20 times, ch 3, sl st in top corner ch sp, *(ch 2, skip next st, sl st in next ch sp) 3 times, sl st in next ch sp on next Panel; repeat from * 9 more times, (ch 2, skip next st, sl st in next ch sp) 2 times, ch 2, skip next st, (sl st, ch 3, sl st) in next top corner ch sp, [ch 2, skip next ch sp, (sl st in next st, ch 2, skip next ch sp) 4 times], ◊(sl st, ch 3, sl st) in next st; repeat between [ ]; repeat from ◊ 2 more times, sl st in next st, ch 3, sl st in next bottom corner ch sp, fasten off.

Sew buttons to first long edge using ch-3 lps on opposite side for buttonholes.

Cut ribbon into 10 pieces each 11½" long. Tie each into bow around 2nd joining ch sp from bottom between Panels. •

American Eagle Pillow

Designed by Sandra Miller Maxfield & Susie Spier Maxfield

Finished Size

Pillow is 16" square not including Ruffle.

Materials

Worsted-weight yarn — 8 oz. blue, 4 oz. each red, white and gold, small amount yellow
○ 2 yds. metallic gold ½" lace
○ 8 yellow 22-mm gemstone stars
○ 4" piece multicolor striped grosgrain ribbon
○ 1" gold patriotic button
○ 12" American flag
○ 16" pillow form
○ Tapestry needle
○ I crochet hook or size needed to obtain gauge.

Gauge

3 dc sts = 1"; 3 dc rows = 2".
Notes: Wind gold into 3 balls. Wind blue, red, and white into 2 balls each.

When changing colors (see page 158), always drop yarn to same side of work. **Do not** carry dropped colors across to next section of same color. Use a separate ball of yarn for each color section. Fasten off at end of each color section.

Work graph (see page 152), from right to left on odd rows and from left to right on even rows. Front of row 1 is right side of work.

Each square on graph equals 1 dc.

Front

Row 1: With blue, ch 52, dc in 4th ch from hook, dc in each ch across, turn (50 dc).
Rows 2-26: Ch 3, dc in each st across changing colors according to graph, turn. At end of last row, fasten off.

Back Side (make 2)

Row 1: With red, ch 27, dc in 4th ch from hook, dc in each ch across, turn, fasten off (25 dc).
Row 2: Join white with sl st in first st, ch 3, dc in each st across, turn.
Rows 3-26: Alternating red and white, repeat row 2. At end of last row, fasten off.
Holding one Back to one side of Front wrong sides together with Front facing you, matching sts and ends of rows, working through both thickness, join blue with sc in first st on Back piece, evenly space 100 more sc around to opposite end of Back piece; holding other Back piece to other side of Front, working through both thicknesses, evenly space 100 more sc around to beginning, join with sl st in first sc, fasten off. Insert pillow form into Back opening.

Ruffles

Rnd 1: Working in **back lps** of joining rnd, join blue with sl st in any corner st, ch 3, (dc, ch 2, 2 dc) in same st, 2 dc in each st around with (2 dc, ch 2, 2 dc) in each corner st, join with sl st in top of ch-3.
Rnd 2: Ch 3, 2 dc in next st, *(2 dc, ch 2, 2 dc) in next ch-2 sp, (dc in next st, 2 dc in next st) across to next ch-2 sp; repeat from * around, join, fasten off.
Rnd 3: Working in **front lps** of joining rnd, join gold with sl st in any corner st, (ch 6, sl st in 4th ch from hook, 2 dc) in same st, skip next 2 sts, (sl st in next st, ch 6, sl st in 4th ch from hook, 2 dc in same st, skip next 2 sts) around, join with sl st in first sl st, fasten off.

Finishing

1: Tack lace around outer edge of pillow in front of gold Ruffle.
2: Glue gemstone stars to Pillow front as shown in photo.
3: Cut one end of striped ribbon into a V-shape; form 1" loop with opposite end. Sew button over 1" loop onto Pillow Front as shown.
4: For talons, with yellow, ch for 12", fasten off. Wrap around flag 6 times; glue to secure. Glue to pillow over tail of eagle as shown. •

American Eagle Pillow

Continued from page 151

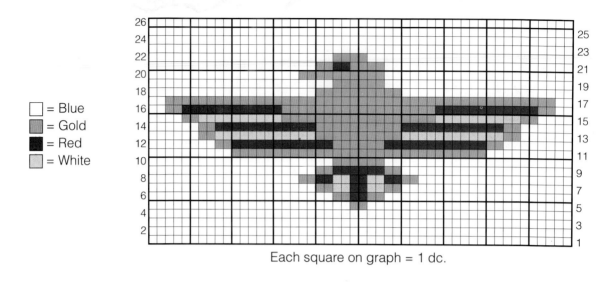

= Blue
= Gold
= Red
= White

Each square on graph = 1 dc.

Watermelon Place Mat and Coaster

Continued from page 133

skip next 4 dc, shell in next dc) 2 times, ch 1, skip next 4 dc on next Square; repeat from * around, join with sl st in top of ch-3, fasten off (20 shells).

Rnd 2: Join red with sc in first shell, *ch 3, sc in next ch-1 sp, (ch 1, 9 dc in next shell, ch 1, sc in next ch-1 sp) 3 times, *(ch 3, sc in next shell, ch 3, sc in next ch-1 sp) 2 times, (ch 1, 9 dc in next shell, ch 1, sc in next ch-1 sp) 3 times; repeat from * around to last shell, ch 3, sc in next shell, ch 3, sc in next ch-1 sp, ch 3, join with

sl st in first sc, fasten off. With black, using Lazy Daisy Stitch (see illustration), embroider **seeds** over red Square according to diagram. •

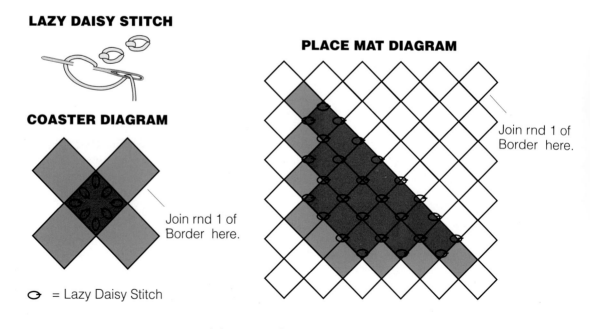

LAZY DAISY STITCH

COASTER DIAGRAM

Join rnd 1 of Border here.

⌀ = Lazy Daisy Stitch

PLACE MAT DIAGRAM

Join rnd 1 of Border here.

Holiday Pillow
Continued from page 144

■ = Green Cross Stitch
▨ = Gold Metallic Cross Stitch
⊟ = Gold Metallic Straight Stitch

Victorian Sleigh

Continued from page 143

canvas between, sl st in each st across, fasten off.

To **shape,** roll one end around index finger, with gray, tack sides of plastic canvas in place.

Assembly

1: Whipstitch (see illustration) plastic canvas Sides and Center together to form sleigh shape. Insert into crocheted Outside. Baste through Center

seam to hold.

2: Sew Runners to bottom of sleigh through plastic canvas having curved ends in front.

3: Place Inside into sleigh. With Outside facing you, using F hook and white, working around upper edge and through both thicknesses, join with sl st in any st, sl st in each st around to close, fasten off.

4: Cut two 20" pieces from bead strand. Tack in place according to dotted lines on diagram.

5: For **bow** (make 2), cut piece

gray ribbon, bead strand and rose ribbon each 18" long. With all pieces held together, fold into 4" bow

6: Tack one bow to center back on top of Sleigh and other to center front on top as shown in photo. •

WHIPSTITCH

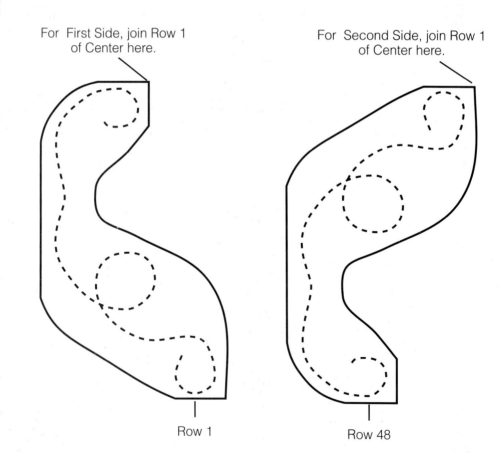

For First Side, join Row 1 of Center here.

For Second Side, join Row 1 of Center here.

Row 1

Row 48

General Instructions

Getting Started

Yarn & Hooks

Always use the weight of yarn specified in the pattern so you can be assured of achieving the proper gauge. It is best to purchase extra of each color needed to allow for differences in tension and dyes.

The hook size stated in the pattern is to be used as a guide. Always work a swatch of the stitch pattern with the suggested hook size. If you find your gauge is smaller or larger than what is specified, choose a different size hook.

Gauge

Gauge is measured by counting the number of rows or stitches per inch. Each of the patterns featured in this book will have a gauge listed. Gauge for some small motifs or flowers is given as an overall measurement. Proper gauge must be attained for the project to come out the size stated, and to prevent ruffling and puckering.

Make a swatch in the stitch indicated in the gauge section of the instructions. Lay the swatch flat and measure the stitches. If you have more stitches per inch than specified in the pattern, your gauge is too tight and you need a larger hook. Fewer stitches per inch indicates a gauge that is too loose. In this case, choose a smaller hook size. Next, check the number of rows. If necessary, adjust your row gauge slightly by pulling the loops down a little tighter on your hook or by pulling the loops up slightly to extend them.

Once you've attained the proper gauge, you're ready to start your project. Remember to check your gauge periodically to avoid problems later.

Pattern Repeat Symbols

Written crochet instructions typically include symbols such as parentheses, asterisks and brackets. In some patterns a diamond or bullet (dot) may be added.

( ) Parentheses enclose instructions which are to be worked again later or the number of times indicated after the parentheses. For example, "(2 dc in next st, skip next st) 5 times" means to follow the instructions within the parentheses a total of five times. If no number appears after the parentheses, you will be instructed when to repeat further into the pattern. Parentheses may also be used to enclose a group of stitches which should be worked in one space or stitch. For example, "(2 dc, ch 2, 2 dc) in next st" means to work all the stitches within the parentheses in the next stitch.

* Asterisks may be used alone or in pairs, usually in combination with parentheses. If used in pairs, the instructions enclosed within asterisks will be followed by instructions for repeating. These repeat instructions may appear later in the pattern or immediately after the last asterisk. For example, "*Dc in next 4 sts, (2 dc, ch 2, 2 dc) in corner sp*, dc in next 4 sts; repeat between ** 2 more times" means to work through the instructions up to the word "repeat," then repeat only the instructions that are enclosed within the asterisks twice.

If used alone, an asterisk marks the beginning of instructions which are to be repeated. Work through the instructions from the beginning, then repeat only the portion after the * up to the word "repeat"; then follow any remaining instructions. If a number of times is given, work through the instructions one time, repeat the number of times stated, then follow the remainder of the instructions.

[ ] Brackets, ◊ diamonds and • bullets are used in the same manner as asterisks. Follow the specific instructions given when repeating.

Finishing

Patterns that require assembly will suggest a tapestry needle in the materials. This should be a #16, #18 or #26 blunt-tipped tapestry needle. When stitching pieces together, be careful to keep the seams flat so pieces do not pucker.

Hiding loose ends is never a fun task, but if done correctly, may mean the difference between an item looking great for years or one that quickly shows signs of wear. Always leave 6-8" of yarn when beginning or ending. Thread the loose end into your tapestry needle and carefully weave through the back of several stitches. Then, weave in the opposite direction, going through different strands. Gently pull the end and clip, allowing the end to pull up under the stitches.

If your project needs blocking, a light steam pressing works well. Lay your project on a large table or on the floor, depending on the size, shaping and smoothing by hand as much as possible. Adjust your steam iron to the permanent press setting, then hold slightly above the stitches, allowing the steam to penetrate the thread. Do not rest the iron on the item. Gently pull and smooth the stitches into shape, spray lightly with starch and allow to dry completely.

Stiffening

There are many liquid products on the market made specifically for stiffening doilies and other soft items. For best results, carefully read the manufacturer's instructions on the product you select before beginning.

Forms for shaping can be many things. Styrofoam® shapes and plastic margarine tubs work well for items such as bowls and baskets. Glass or plastic drinking glasses are used for vase-type items. If you cannot find an item with the dimensions given in the pattern to use as a form, any similarly sized item can be shaped by adding layers of plastic wrap. Place the dry crochet piece over the form to check the fit, remembering that it will stretch when wet.

For shaping flat pieces, corrugated cardboard,

Styrofoam® or a cutting board designed for sewing may be used. Be sure to cover all surfaces of forms or blocking board with clear plastic wrap, securing with cellophane tape.

If you have not used fabric stiffener before, you may wish to practice on a small swatch before stiffening the actual item. For proper saturation when using conventional stiffeners, work liquid thoroughly into the crochet piece and let stand for about 15 minutes. Then, squeeze out excess stiffener and blot with paper towels. Continue to blot while shaping to remove as much stiffener as possible. Stretch over form, shape and pin with rust proof pins; allow to dry, then unpin.

For More Information

Sometimes even the most experienced needlecrafters can find themselves having trouble following instructions. If you have difficulty completing your project, write to:

Crochet Holiday Collection
The Needlecraft Shop
23 Old Pecan Road
Big Sandy, Texas 75755

Stitch Guide

Basic Stitches

Front Loop (a)/Back Loop (b)
(front lp/back lp)

Chain (ch)
Yo, draw hook through lp.

Slip Stitch (sl st)
Insert hook in st, yo, draw through st and lp on hook.

Single Crochet (sc)
Insert hook in st (a), yo, draw lp through, yo, draw through both lps on hook (b).

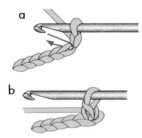

Standard Stitch Abbreviations

ch(s)	chain(s)
dc	double crochet
dtr	double treble crochet
hdc	half double crochet
lp(s)	loop(s)
rnd(s)	round(s)
sc	single crochet
sl st	slip stitch
sp(s)	space(s)
st(s)	stitch(es)
tog	together
tr	treble crochet
ttr	triple treble crochet
yo	yarn over

Half Double Crochet (hdc)
Yo, insert hook in st (a), yo, draw lp through (b), yo, draw through all 3 lps on hook (c).

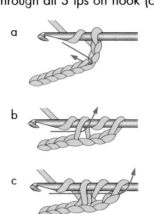

Double Crochet (dc)
Yo, insert hook in st (a), yo, draw lp through (b), (yo, draw through 2 lps on hook) 2 times (c and d).

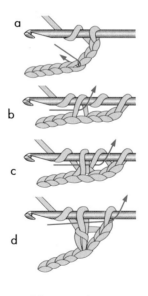

Treble Crochet (tr)
Yo 2 times, insert hook in st, yo, draw lp through, (yo, draw through 2 lps on hook) 3 times.

Final Step

Double Treble Crochet (dtr)
Yo 3 times, insert hook in st, yo, draw lp through, (yo, draw through 2 lps on hook) 4 times.

Final Step

Triple Treble Crochet (ttr)
Yo 4 times, insert hook in st, yo, draw lp through, (yo, draw through 2 lps on hook) 5 times.

Final Step

Changing Colors

Single Crochet Color Change
(sc color change)
Drop first color; yo with 2nd color, draw through last 2 lps of st.

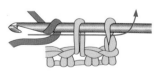

Double Crochet Color Change
(dc color change)
Drop first color; yo with 2nd color, draw through last 2 lps of st.

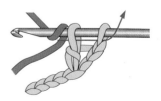

Reverse Single Crochet (reverse sc)

Working from left to right, insert hook in next st to the right (a), yo, draw through st, complete as sc (b).

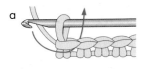

Sc Over Ring

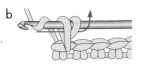

Whipstitch
is used to join two or more pieces together.

Decreasing

Single Crochet next 2 stitches together (sc next 2 sts tog)
Draw up lp in each of next 2 sts, yo, draw through all 3 lps on hook.

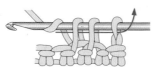

Half Double Crochet next 2 stitches together (hdc next 2 sts tog)
(Yo, insert hook in next st, yo, draw lp through) 2 times, yo, draw through all 5 lps on hook.

Double Crochet next 2 stitches together (dc next 2 sts tog)
(Yo, insert hook in next st, yo, draw lp through, yo, draw through 2 lps on hook) 2 times, yo, draw through all 3 lps on hook.

Special Stitches

Front Post/Back Post Stitches (fp/bp)
Yo, insert hook from front to back (a) or back to front (b) around post of st on indicated row; complete as stated in pattern.

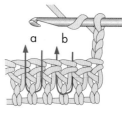

Afghan Knit Stitch

Knit #1
Knit #2
Knit #3
Knit #4

Embroidery Stitches

Backstitch

Straight Stitch

Outline Stitch

Back Bar of sc

French Knot

Satin Stitch

The patterns in this book are written using American crochet stitch terminology. For our international customers, hook sizes, stitches and yarn definitions should be converted as follows:

US	= UK
sl st (slip stitch)	= sc (single crochet)
sc (single crochet)	= dc (double crochet)
hdc (half double crochet)	= htr (half treble crochet)
dc (double crochet)	= tr (treble crochet)
tr (treble crochet)	= dtr (double treble crochet)
dtr (double treble crochet)	= ttr (triple treble crochet)
skip	= miss

Thread/Yarns

Bedspread Weight	= No.10 Cotton or Virtuoso
Sport Weight	= 4 Ply or thin DK
Worsted Weight	= Thick DK or Aran

Crochet Hooks

Metric	US
.60mm	14
.75mm	12
1.00mm	10
1.50mm	6
1.75mm	5
2.00mm	B/1
2.50mm	C/2
3.00mm	D/3
3.50mm	E/4
4.00mm	F/5
4.50mm	G/6
5.00mm	H/8
5.50mm	I/9
6.00mm	J/10

Measurements

1"	=	2.54 cm
1 yd.	=	.9144 m
1 oz.	=	28.35 g

But, as with all patterns, test your gauge (tension) to be sure.

Pattern Index

Designer Index